22207
-45

R48015

D1523597

K

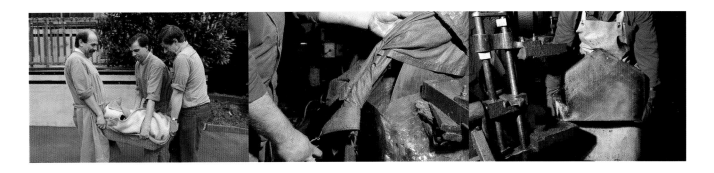

Für Philipp

REFLEXIONEN IN STEIN

BERND MUNSTEINER

REFLECTIONS IN STONE

WILHELM LINDEMANN (ED.)

ARNOLDSCHE

TABLE OF CONTENTS

INHALTSVERZEICHNIS

»DENN ALLE LUST WILL EWIGKEIT«[1]
Bernd Munsteiner – Reflexionen in Stein

›FOR ALL DELIGHT WANTS ETERNITY‹[1]
Bernd Munsteiner – Reflections in Stone

Wilhelm Lindemann

Im Urteil von Fachleuten und Sammlern gilt Bernd Munsteiner nicht nur als der Neuerer des Edelsteinschliffs – er gilt vor allem als der erste zeitgenössische Künstler, der ausschließlich mit Mineralien arbeitet. Dieses umgangssprachlich zumeist als »Edelsteine« bezeichnete Material ist Ausgangs- und Zielpunkt seines künstlerischen Schaffens.[2] Der Versuch einer kunst- und kulturhistorischen Verortung seines Werks führt daher zwangsläufig auch zu eher allgemeinen Überlegungen über die Geschichte der Verwendung von kristallinen Mineralien in Kunst und Kunsthandwerk.

In historischer Zeit konnte sich kaum ein Betrachter der auratischen Wirkung der Kristalle entziehen. Bereits die antiken Quellen schenken ihren magisch-medizinischen, wirtschaftlichen und verarbeitungstechnischen oder auch naturwissenschaftlich-mineralogischen Aspekten große Aufmerksamkeit. Wenn es allerdings um die spezifisch

»Augustuskameo« vom Aachener Lotharkreuz, antiker Kameo, Kreuz um 980, Domschatz-
kammer, Aachen/D ‖ ›Augustus Cameo‹, from the Cross of Lothar, Aachen, ancient cameo,
cross ca 980, Cathedral Treasury, Aachen/D

In the estimation of both specialists and collectors, Bernd Munsteiner has not merely revolutionised gem-cutting – he is known above all as the first contemporary artist to work exclusively with minerals. This material, usually designated ›precious stones‹ in colloquial terms, is the alpha and omega of his creative work as an artist.[2] Consequently, any attempt at locating where his work is in terms of art and cultural history must of necessity lead to general thoughts on the history of the use of crystalline minerals in the fine and the decorative arts.

In historical times, hardly anyone who saw them could resist the aural impact made by crystals. Ancient sources were already paying close attention to their magic, medical and economic properties and the techniques for working them as well as their scientific and mineralogical sides. However, where the specifically aesthetic qualities of the material *per se* are concerned or the questions arising from them of how it is to be aesthetically worked to turn it into art, the relevant sources have tended, and rather surprisingly so, to remain mute to the present day. Only a 1992 exhibition in Darmstadt, *Faszination Edelstein [The Fascination of Gems]* has been devoted to

working out the myth in terms of its historical aspects.[3] We do know that the sparkle of gems is fascinating. Why, however, should their sparkle be considered beautiful? In the following some thoughts on a genealogy of beauty in stone will be discussed as a preamble to a closer look at Bernd Munsteiner's work.

FROM THE BEAUTIFUL SACROSANCT TO SECULAR BEAUTY

Much suggests that the aura surrounding gems – which often surpasses that of gold – derived first of all from the specific magic properties attributed to each of them. Even people in early cultures assigned a symbolic meaning to unworked, isolated boulders (*Findlinge*: usually large clasts in the geological sense) which had a distinctive form or colour as representing powers from the spirit world or as monuments to human experience of emergencies. These early people made artefacts of stone as sacral objects or as fetishes endowed with very earthly powers. Or they viewed them as potent messengers from a totemistic cosmology which informed whoever owned them about what his place in the world was. Glittering coloured stones were invested by our prehistoric forebears with a sacred aura and this magic significance of gemstones certainly remained the chief reason for their use on into the 16th century AD.[4] Even today gemstones are thought to bring good luck or misfortune as is shown by the growing band of those who adhere to esoteric lore in the belief that such stones have healing properties.

However, even Greco-Roman antiquity saw the development of the first criteria for evaluating gemstones apart from sacral and magic functions. Pliny the Elder, the author of a standard work on gemstones which remained authoritative on into the Renaissance,[5] did his best to establish almost scientific categories for minerals and also tried to represent their economic aspects.[6] The aura and aesthetic qualities of stones were only marginally noticed by Pliny the Elder. He pointed out their enormous importance to both religious and profane cults, criticising the indulgence of luxury associated with particularly valuable stones. Apart from their size and the rarity with which they came on the market, he considered

hardness the most important constituent of value. Like other ancient authors, he regarded the ›unconquerable‹ *adámas* (diamond in Greek) as the most valuable gemstone.

Another criterion for quality mentioned by Pliny is effulgence – radiance (Lat. *fulgor*) – only attained by pure crystals. ›Little clouds‹ and other ›impurities‹ in a crystal only lessened its transparency (the quality of transmitting light without diffusion) and its capacity for reflecting light it cast and were, therefore, in his opinion flaws which reduced its value.[7] This judgement, questionable as it is in terms of aesthetics, that high quality must always mean flawless (or ›of the first water‹) has persisted on the market to the present day: because minerals meeting the standards applied to the criterion of flawlessness have always been relatively difficult to come by, the law that purity must epitomize value-enhancing quality has prevailed. Purity and clarity of colour were, therefore, first linked with high market value and, surely at the same time, with the concept of beauty. However, until the rapidly turning cutting wheel was introduced in the 15th century, cutting and polishing

ästhetischen Qualitäten des Materials an sich oder um die daraus resultierenden Fragen der kunstvollen Bearbeitung geht, bleibt die einschlägige Literatur bis auf den heutigen Tag zumeist auf eine merkwürdige Weise sprachlos. Lediglich die Darmstädter Ausstellung *Faszination Edelstein* aus dem Jahr 1992 widmete sich auch der Herausbildung des Mythos unter kunsthistorischen Aspekten.[3] Wir wissen zwar, dass Edelsteine faszinierend funkeln. Warum aber wird dieses Funkeln auch für schön gehalten? Nachfolgend sollen einige Überlegungen zu einer Genealogie des Schönen im Stein angestellt werden, bevor eine Annäherung an das Werk Bernd Munsteiners versucht wird.

VOM SCHÖNEN HEILIGEN ZUR SÄKULAREN SCHÖNHEIT

Vieles spricht dafür, dass sich die Aura der Edelsteine – die die des Goldes oft noch übertrifft – zunächst hauptsächlich aus den unterschiedlichen magischen Kräften hergeleitet hat, die man ihnen jeweils zuschrieb. Schon die Menschen früher Kulturen wiesen steinernen Findlingen mit einer besonderen Form oder Farbe symbolische Bedeutungen als Repräsentanten der jenseitigen Mächte oder als Denkmale einer menschlichen Kontingenzerfahrung zu. Sie fertigten Artefakte aus Stein als sakrale Objekte oder als Fetische mit sehr diesseitigen Potenzen. Oder sie sahen in ihnen wirkmächtige Boten aus einer totemistischen Kosmologie, die ihrem jeweiligen Eigentümer Auskunft über seinen Ort in der Welt gaben. Glitzernde, farbige Steine wurden bereits von unseren prähistorischen Vorfahren mit der Aura des Heiligen versehen, und sicher blieb diese magische Bedeutung der Edelsteine bis ins 16. Jahrhundert der Hauptgrund für ihre Verwendung.[4] Bis auf den heutigen Tag bringen Edelsteine in den Augen der Menschen Glück oder Unglück oder haben, wie die wachsende Anhängerschaft esoterischer Lehren glaubt, heilende Kräfte.

Allerdings entwickelten sich schon in der Antike erste Bewertungskriterien für Edelsteine jenseits der sakralen und magischen Funktionen. Plinius d. Ä., Verfasser des noch bis in die Renaissance hinein gültigen antiken Standardwerks zu den Edelsteinen[5], bemühte sich um eine fast naturwissenschaftliche Kategorisierung der Mineralien sowie um die Darstellung ihrer ökonomischen Aspekte.[6] Aura und ästhetische Qualität der Steine fanden bei Plinius d. Ä. nur eine eher mittelbare Beachtung. Er stellte die große Bedeutung im religiösen und profanen Kult heraus und kritisierte den Luxus, der mit besonders wertvollen Steinen getrieben wurde. Als wichtige Konstituente des Wertes von Edelsteinen betrachtete er neben der Größe und der Seltenheit des Vorkommens am Markt in erster Linie ihre Härte. Der »unbezwingbare« *Adamas* (Diamant) galt ihm wie auch anderen Autoren der Antike als der Wertvollste.

Als ein weiteres Qualitätskriterium erwähnt Plinius den Glanz (lat. *fulgor*), den nur die reinen Kristalle erreichen. »Wölkchen« und andere »Verunreinigungen« im Kristall stehen der Lichttransparenz und -reflexion im Wege und sind deshalb für ihn ein wertmindernder Makel.[7] Dieses in ästhetischer Hinsicht eher fragwürdige Verdikt, dass hohe Qualität stets makellos (bzw. »lupenrein«) sein muss, hat bis heute am Markt Gültigkeit: Weil Mineralien, die dem Kriterium der Makellosigkeit entsprechen, vergleichsweise selten erhältlich waren (und sind), hat sich das Reinheitsverdikt als das wertsteigernde Qualitätskriterium schlechthin durchgesetzt. Reinheit und klare Farbe werden also zunächst mit einem hohen Marktwert verknüpft und sicher gleichzeitig auch mit dem Begriff Schönheit korreliert. Allerdings war bis zur Einführung des schnell drehenden Schleifrades im 15. Jahrhundert ein Schleifen und Polieren von Steinen, insbesondere von Diamanten, zur Erzielung einer Brillanz im heutigen Sinne technisch noch nicht möglich. Zudem stand vor der Erfindung der Lupe »Reinheit« für das mit bloßem Auge erkennbare Qualitätsmerkmal. Aus den mühsam durch Reiben von Hand polierten Steinen schimmerte zumeist nur ein eher matt glänzendes Feuer.

Nur sehr reiche und mächtige Würdenträger[8] konnten sich in der Regel mit den durch diese Bearbeitung wertvoll gewordenen Steinen schmücken. Bestimmte Steine waren im spätantiken Byzanz sogar ausdrücklich dem kaiserlichen Hof vorbehalten.[9] Die Aura der Steine und die ihrer Träger verschmolzen, und die Steine wurden zum Zeichen religiöser

links: Das mit 12 Edelsteinen verzierte Himmlische Jerusalem, vor 1350, Herzog-August-Bibliothek, Wolfenbüttel/D ‖ **left:** The Heavenly Jerusalem, decorated with 12 gems, before 1350, Herzog August Library, Wolfenbüttel/D ‖ **rechts:** Reliquiar, Bergkristall, Kupfer vergoldet, Steinbesatz, Rheinland, um 1200, Schnütgenmuseum, Köln/D ‖ **right:** Reliquary, rock crystal, copper-gilt, set with stones, Rhineland, ca 1200, Schnütgenmuseum, Cologne/D

stones, especially diamonds, to attain brilliancy in today's sense of the word was impossible. Moreover, before the magnifying glass was invented, ›purity‹ was a quality that had to be judged by the naked eye alone. A matt sheen instead of fire was all that could be elicited by the strenuous process of rubbing hand-polished stones.

Only very rich and powerful dignitaries[8] could, as a rule, adorn themselves with the stones which had assumed value through such treatment. In Byzantium in late antiquity, some stones were reserved expressly for the imperial court.[9] The aura of stones and that of their wearers fused and the stones became a sign of both spiritual and temporal power and glory. Consequently, by late antiquity and the early Middle Ages, gemstones figured prominently as the materials of choice for gracing the insignia worn by the representatives of ecclesiastical and secular authority. Gemstones adorned crowns, sceptres, rings and receptacles for profane and especially sacral use.[10]

The use of gemstones on the implements and utensils sacred to Christian ritual – in particular on chalices, monstrances, tabernacles or reliquaries (ill. p. 17) – introduced the next and definitely crucial stage in the history of their becoming loaded with aural connotations, in which they themselves became the mystic symbol of the divine or sacred. The advent of St Augustine of Hippo (354–430) and the end of Early Christian iconoclasm ushered in the conception of nature mirroring the divine Creator and an artist's works standing for the artist: ›Those who know can now read these references in their natural environment as in a book and receive information on God and his plan for the salvation of mankind. The divine revelation in the books of the Bible must be similarly interpreted. As in the writings of Greco-Roman antiquity, a »sensus spiritualis« was seen in the Bible as well which transcended literal interpretation. Gemstones are mentioned in all sorts of passages in the Bible.‹[11] To take one example, twelve gemstones bearing the names of the tribes of Israel in the breastplate to be worn by the High Priest (Exodus 29, 8–21), prefigure the twelve Apostles, ›all manner of precious stones garnish the foundations of the walls‹ of the Heavenly city in Revelation (Revelation 21,19–21; ill. p. 17), decorate

oder weltlicher Macht und Herrlichkeit. Bereits in der Spätantike und im frühen Mittelalter gehörten Edelsteine daher zu den bevorzugten Ausstattungsmaterialien der Insignien kirchlicher und weltlicher Würdenträger. Sie zierten Kronen, Zepter, Ringe, profane und vor allem sakrale Behältnisse.[10]

Die Verwendung von Edelsteinen an den sakralen Geräten des christlichen Ritus – insbesondere an Messkelchen, Monstranzen, Tabernakeln oder Reliquiaren (Abb. S. 17) – leitete die nächste und sicher entscheidende Etappe in der Geschichte ihrer auratischen Aufladung ein, in der sie selbst zum mystischen Sinnbild des Göttlichen bzw. des Heiligen wurden. Mit Augustinus (345–430) und nach dem Ende des frühchristlichen Bilderverbotes verbreitete sich die Auffassung, dass die Natur auf den göttlichen Schöpfer verweise wie das Werk auf den Künstler: »Der Kundige kann nun in der ihn umgebenden Natur diese Verweise wie in einem Buch lesen und Informationen über Gott und seinen Heilsplan erhalten. Ebenso bedarf die Offenbarung Gottes in den Büchern der Bibel einer Deutung. Wie schon in den antiken Schriften wurde auch in der Bibel ein ›sensus spiritualis‹ gesehen, der über die wörtliche Auslegung hinausgeht. Edelsteine werden nun in der Bibel an den verschiedensten Stellen erwähnt.«[11] So zieren zum Beispiel zwölf Edelsteine mit den Namen der Stämme Israels den Brustschild des Hohen Priesters (Exodus 28,15–21), verweisen auf die zwölf Apostel, krönen in der Offenbarung des Johannes die Mauern des himmlischen Jerusalem (Apokalypse 21,17–20; Abb. S. 17), schmücken den Thron Gottes oder zieren das Tor zum Paradies (Apokalypse 4,2–3 und 4,6). Sie verweisen bildhaft auf die Herrlichkeit Gottes. Der Bergkristall beispielsweise wurde als eine Form der Inkarnation Christi interpretiert, den unterschiedlichen Edelsteinen wurden bestimmte christliche Tugenden zugeordnet. Auf die Edelsteine als kostbarste Teile eines christlichen sakralen Objekts (etwa einer Monstranz oder eines Reliquiars), ging – durch die räumliche Nähe – auch die immaterielle Symbolkraft des Allerheiligsten, des »Leibes Jesu«, oder der Reliquie über.[12]

Im ästhetischen Empfinden und Denken des Mittelalters, das noch tief in die Renaissancekunst hinein wirkte, war die unmittelbare Zusammengehörigkeit von Schönheit und

Tugendhaftigkeit selbstverständlich. Das Heilige wurde auch als das Schöne betrachtet. Die leuchtenden Edelsteine in den sakralen Objekten mussten dem gläubigen Betrachter als Sinnbilder des Göttlichen oder Heiligen auch besonders schön erscheinen. Die verfeinerten Schleiftechniken im ausgehenden Mittelalter (u.a. im frühen Facettenschliff) ermöglichten es zudem, die planmäßige Herstellung eines funkelnden, vermeintlich dem Stein innewohnenden Lichts zum zentralen Anliegen der Edelsteingestalter zu machen. Sie bedienten damit eine alte, bereits vorchristliche Vorstellung, welche alle Phänomene des Lichts wie Sonne, Blitz usw. als Sinnbilder des Göttlichen oder als Erscheinung der Gottheit selbst verstand. Das für den »Unwissenden« auf geheimnisvolle Weise zustande kommende Licht war im Mittelalter nicht nur zum Sinnbild der Gottheit, sondern zugleich zur Verkörperung des Schönen und Guten geworden. Der emotionale Affekt beim gläubigen Betrachter geschliffener Edelsteine in sakralen Objekten musste sich nun in dem Maße bis zur mystischen Verzückung steigern, in dem Edelsteine begannen, das göttliche Licht zu repräsentieren.[13]

Mittelbar bereitete dieser Prozess aber auch die Herausbildung eines profanen Schönheitsideals vor. Spätestens mit dem 14. Jahrhundert, mit der zunehmenden Etablierung eines künstlerischen Subjekts, das sich selbst als Schöpfer definiert, entstand eine erste Vorstellung vom »schönen Werk«. Noch handelte es sich um ein Abbild göttlicher Schönheit im Sinne eines Versuchs der Aussöhnung Gottes mit der in irdischer Gottverlorenheit auf Erlösung harrenden Menschheit. Der Literaturwissenschaftler Spoerri macht im Hinblick auf die Dichtkunst Petrarcas eine Bemerkung, die auch für die Entwicklung des Edelsteinschliffs sehr zutreffend erscheint: »Gerade hier geschieht eine der wichtigsten Wendungen der europäischen Geschichte. Der ungeheure Akzent, der nun auf den Einzelnen fällt und ihn in seiner Vereinzelung die Innerlichkeit entdecken lässt, – damit auch den Zwiespalt zwischen innen und außen, zwischen Subjekt und Objekt – äußert sich in einem neuen Verhältnis zum Wort [oder zum Bild]. Das Wort [oder Bild] wird zu einem Ding an sich. Als einziges Vehikel

God's throne or adorn the gates of Paradise (Revelation 4,2–3 and 4,6). They refer symbolically to the glory of God. Rock crystal, for instance, was interpreted as a form of the Incarnation (and the Immaculate Conception). The dematerialised symbolic powers of the Most Holy, the ›body of Christ‹, or a sacred relic were transferred – via physical propinquity – to gemstones as the most precious parts of Christian sacral objects (such as a monstrance or a reliquary).[12]

According to medieval aesthetics and thinking, which prevailed far into the Renaissance, the immediate connection between beauty and virtue was a matter of course. What was holy was also regarded as beautiful. The gemstones glowing in sacral objects must have appeared particularly beautiful as the symbols of the divine or holy to the devout worshippers gazing on them. The more sophisticated techniques of cutting stones introduced in the late Middle Ages (including early cutting into facets) also made it possible to plan for the sparkling light effects presumed to be inherent in a stone and to make them the main concern of those working with gemstones. They were, therefore, making use of a pre-Christian idea, according to which all phenomena associated with light, such as the sun, lightning, etc, were conceived of as symbolizing the divine or the epiphany of the divine. In the Middle Ages, the light which was thus made to appear so mysteriously to ›those who knew not‹ both symbolised divinity and embodied what was good and beautiful. The emotional impact made on a devout worshipper looking at cut gemstones in sacral objects was bound to be elevated to the heights of mystic rapture when gemstones began to represent the divine light.[13]

This process also indirectly affected the formation of a profane ideal of beauty. From the 14th century at the latest, with the artist beginning to emerge as an individual defining himself as a creator, a demiurge, ideas of what constituted a ›beautiful work‹ surfaced. This was still an ectype of divine beauty in the sense that it represented an attempt at reconciling God with humankind which persisted in earth-bound impiety while awaiting redemption. Theophil Spoerri, a specialist in comparative literature, has made an observation about Petrarch's poetry which also seems apposite to the development of gem-cutting: ›This is where one of the most important turns taken by European history occurred. The enormous emphasis which now fell upon the individual, making him in his solitude discover his inner being – and, therefore, also the discrepancy between inside and out, between subject and object – is expressed in a new relationship with the word [or with the picture]. As the only vehicle for subjectivity the word [or picture] is reified. It gives the individual, who is conscious of his solitude and transience, the means of creating a whole, something imperishable – beauty as secularised sanctity.‹[14]

In the Renaissance, the development of gem-cutting culminated in faceting. As a secular symbol of sanctity, it has maintained this symbolic power from the High Renaissance on down to the present day, bringing forth the ideal type of the ›beautiful gemstone‹. Nowadays everyone associates this ideal type with the concept like a formalised logo. Moreover, Spoerri's observation sounds like the inspiration for the advertising campaign launched by the DeBeers monopoly addressing the permanence of diamonds.

An iconography of the beautifully cut gemstone did not arise concomitantly with the transition from the late Middle Ages to the Renaissance as an autochthonous principle. In any case, relevant sources are lacking. Nevertheless, gem-cutting developed in such major Renaissance centres as Venice, Milan and Florence in northern Italy and Bruges in Flanders in immediate proximity to the other arts and sciences – exemplified by the systematic training in the *pietre dure* technique promoted by the Medicis in Florence. All too striking are the – if the analogy is permissible – mathematical, aesthetic and symbolic links between gem-cutting in facets and the architecture of the age. By the Middle Ages the question of light – especially in ecclesiastical architecture – had begun to assume major significance. The windows invisible to visitors in the octagon above the central crossing of Romanesque cathedrals focus light – representing the divine principle – over the empty sanctuary, where the altar is. At the same time, the polygonal architecture of the central structure, taking up the problem of squaring the circle, unresolved since antiquity, is a reference to the Christian metaphor for the infinity of God.[15]

Francesco Ferrucci (?), »Vase mit Blumen«, Mosaik aus Halbedelsteinen in der *Pietre dure*-Technik, Florenz, frühes 17. Jahrhundert, Privatbesitz London/GB ‖ Francesco Ferrucci (?), ›Vase of Flowers‹, mosaic of semiprecious stones in the *pietre dure* technique, Florence, early 17th century, private collection, London/GB

der Subjektivität gibt es dem Einzelnen, der sich seiner Vereinzelung und Vergänglichkeit bewusst wird, das Mittel, ein Ganzes und Unvergängliches zu schaffen – Schönheit als säkularisierte Heiligkeit.«[14]

Der am Ende der Entwicklung des Edelsteinschliffs in der Renaissance stehende Facettenschliff hat als säkulares Sinnbild des Heiligen diese Symbolkraft von der Hochrenaissance bis zum heutigen Tag behauptet und den Idealtypus des »schönen Edelsteines« hervorgebracht, den heutzutage jedermann wie ein formalisiertes Logo mit diesem Begriff verbindet. Spoerris Bemerkung könnte darüber hinaus sogar die Werbekampagne des Diamanten-Multis DeBeers, die die Unvergänglichkeit der Diamanten anspricht, geradezu inspiriert haben.

Eine neuzeitliche Ikonographie des schön geschliffenen Edelsteines hatte sich mit dem Übergang vom ausgehenden Mittelalter zur Renaissance nicht als autochthones Gestaltungsprinzip herausgebildet. Jedenfalls fehlen entsprechende Quellen. Allerdings entwickelte sich der Edelsteinschliff in den Renaissance-Metropolen Norditaliens (Venedig, Mailand und Florenz) oder Flanderns (Brügge) in unmittelbarer räumlicher Nachbarschaft zu den übrigen Künsten und Wissenschaften – wie beispielsweise die von den Medicis mit System geförderte Ausbildung in der *Pietre dure*-Technik in Florenz zeigt (Abb. S. 20). Allzu augenfällig – insofern sei die Analogie erlaubt – sind die mathematischen, ästhetischen und symbolischen Bezüge im einsetzenden Facettenschliff zur Architektur der Epoche. Bereits im Mittelalter begann die Frage des Lichts – insbesondere im Kirchenbau – eine zentrale Bedeutung zu entwickeln. Die für den Besucher unsichtbaren Fenster in dem achteckigen Polygon über der zentralen Vierung der romanischen Dome fokussieren das Licht – das göttliche Prinzip repräsentierend – über dem leeren Altarraum. Gleichzeitig verweist die polygonale Architektur des Zentralbaus, das seit der Antike ungelöste Problem der Quadratur des Kreises aufnehmend, auf die christliche Metapher für den unendlichen Gott.[15] Das Polyeder wurde in der Renaissancekunst zum Sinnbild der Unendlichkeit schlechthin.[16]

Die humanistischen Philosophen der frühen Renaissance gingen – auf dem Weg zur Profanierung des Schönheitskultes – den weiter oben bereits für die Kunst aufgezeigten Weg der Subjekt-Objekt-Aufspaltung einen Gedankenschritt weiter, indem sie dem erkennenden Ich die Möglichkeit der Teilhabe am göttlichen Wesen durch Erleuchtung zuerkannten. Ficino (1433–1499), der am Hof der Medici in unmittelbarer Nachbarschaft zu den bedeutenden Künstlern der Florentiner Renaissance arbeitende Begründer des modernen Neuplatonismus, formulierte: »Daher ist das Licht, was immer es sieht, nichts anderes als eine Ausweitung der reinen und wirksamen geistigen Form. Wo also die Reinheit und Wirksamkeit der Form nicht im Geringsten begrenzt wird, dort strömt das unendliche Licht, von dort breitet sich ein unermessliches Licht aus. Was in den Körpern Sichtbarkeit ist, das ist Klarsicht in den Geistern. Was wiederum in den Körpern sichtbares

In Renaissance art, the polyhedron became the ultimate symbol of infinity.[16]

In acknowledging the possibility that the conscious self might share in the divine being through enlightenment, the humanist philosophers of the Early Renaissance went a step further – towards secularising the cult of beauty – in their thinking on the way outlined above respecting art as far as the split between subject and object was concerned. Marsilio Ficino (1433–1499), who, as the founder of Neo-Platonism in the modern age, lived at the Medici court close to the important artists of the Florentine Renaissance, put this in the following terms: ›Consequently, whatever it sees, light is nothing other than an expansion of pure and effectively spiritual form. Where, therefore, purity and effectiveness of form are not limited in the slightest, there infinite light pours out, hence immeasurable light spreads. Clarity of vision in the spirit is as visibility in bodies. Seeing, in turn, is to the spirit as light is visible in bodies. That is why bodies which come closer to spirit radiate more easily and abundantly and, conversely, what is radiant of its own accord disseminates a spiritual quality about it. Therefore the highest spirit dwells in the highest light and seeing. In it clarity and seeing are the same.‹ [17]

Until faceting had been consistently developed in the Renaissance, light played a role in the aura of a beautiful stone which was closely linked with the natural radiance of the translucent substance. Since cutting techniques were still quite underdeveloped, artisans had to limit themselves to rubbing stones into rounded shapes (cabochons) and polishing them (caboching or cabossing then applied to heraldry in 18th-century English) so that the usually scant light reflected solely due to the crystal structure of the mineral seemed to come from within the stone. Whereas until then the light thus shining out so mysteriously – as a rule reflecting the candlelight in a sacral room – referred directly to the divine principle, the multiple reflections from the facets of a diamond cut by human hand created a restlessly flickering light. The more sophisticated the process of faceting became and, therefore, the way the handling of light determined the external appearance of a stone, the less important became the material as such, which had previously been the sacred substance of the stone itself. The more light assumed the chief function of

links: Hans Schäufelein, »Theuerdank wird durch Fürwittig verleitet, seine Geschicklichkeit an einem Schleifstein zu erproben«, Holzschnitt auf Pergament, 1517 ‖ **left:** Hans Schäufelein, ›Theuerdank is induced by Fürwittig to test his skill at a cutting wheel‹, woodcut on vellum, 1517 ‖
rechts: »Der Steinschneider«, Schleifvorrichtung mit Fußantrieb, 1568 ‖ **right:** ›The Gem-Cutter‹, cutting wheel, foot-powered, 1568

Licht ist, ist in den Geistern Schauen. Deshalb strahlen die Körper, die näher an den Geist herankommen, leichter und reichlicher zurück, und umgekehrt, was alleine strahlt, verbreitet geistige Qualität um sich. Also wohnt im höchsten Geist höchstes Licht und Schauen. In ihm sind Klarheit und Schauen dasselbe.« [17]

Bis zur konsequenten Entwicklung des Facettenschliffs in der Renaissance spielte das Licht in der Aura des schönen Steins eine Rolle, die stark gekoppelt war an die natürliche Leuchtkraft des luziden Materials. Als Folge der noch wenig entwickelten Schleiftechnik beschränkte man sich zumeist auf das Rundreiben und Polieren der Steine (Muggeln), so dass das ausschließlich aufgrund der kristallinen Struktur des Minerals zumeist spärlich reflektierte Licht aus dem Inneren des Steins zu kommen schien. Während bis *dato* dieses geheimnisvoll herausscheinende Licht – in der Regel die Reflexion des Kerzenscheins eines sakralen Raumes – unmittelbar auf das göttliche Prinzip verwies, erzeugten die multiplen Lichtreflexionen an den von Menschenhand erzeugten Facetten des Brillanten ein unruhig flimmerndes Licht. Je differenzierter sich der Prozess der Facettierung und damit der das äußere Erscheinungsbild des Steins bestimmende Umgang mit dem Licht entwickelte, desto geringer wurde die Bedeutung des Materials, die vormals heilige Substanz des Steins selbst. Je mehr das Licht die zentrale Bedeutung gebende Funktion beim geschliffenen Stein einnahm, desto entmaterialisierter erschien das geschliffene Material. Der magische Sinn des Minerals wanderte quasi als irisierender Lichtreflex aus dem Innern auf die facettierte Oberfläche. Mit der Trennung der äußeren Form vom Material begann das Mineral seine stoffgebundene magische Aura zu verlieren. Der Übergang zum säkularen Kult des Schönen stand bevor.

Erst die planmäßige, technische und wiederholbare Herstellung regelmäßiger Facetten machte in der Edelsteinbearbeitung das Licht also selbst zu dem Thema, das den Umgang mit den Edelsteinen regelrecht revolutionieren sollte. Zugleich bereitete der Facettenschliff den massenhaften Einsatz von Schmucksteinen in der Neuzeit vor, indem er mit dem Brillanten den Prototypen des »schönen Edelsteines« definierte und dabei die wissenschaftlich fundierte Wegbeschreibung zu seiner Herstellung mitlieferte. Bei der Facettierung von Edelsteinen, der Herstellung regelmäßiger spiegelnder Flächen unter Anwendung der optischen Gesetze, ging es, physikalisch ausgedrückt, um die Erzeugung einer als Spiegelung virtuellen und insofern transzendentalen Lichtquelle. Auf der Symbolebene entsprach dies einer ästhetischen Zusammenführung des göttlichen Prinzips mit der menschlichen Vernunft. Das darin enthaltene auratische Potenzial wurde durch einen anderen Umstand noch zusätzlich verstärkt: Härte und Kälte des Minerals, insbesondere des wegen seiner Härte Ewigkeit verheißenden Diamanten – Eigenschaften also, die dieses Feuer dem haptischen Zugriff des Menschen entziehen – machten das Licht umso geheimnisvoller. Die haptische Entrücktheit multiplizierte den emotionalen Affekt bei der optischen Wahrnehmung. Die Bannung

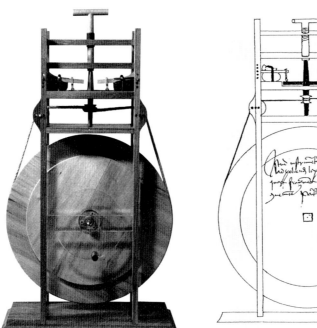
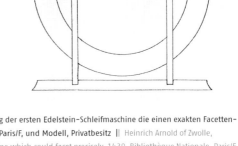

Heinrich Arnold aus Zwolle, Konstruktionszeichnung der ersten Edelstein-Schleifmaschine die einen exakten Facetten-schliff ermöglichte, 1439, Bibliothèque Nationale, Paris/F, und Modell, Privatbesitz ‖ Heinrich Arnold of Zwolle, construction drawing of the first gem-cutting machine which could facet precisely, 1439, Bibliothèque Nationale, Paris/F and model, private collection

giving meaning to the cut stone, the more dematerialised did the cut material seem. The magic significance of the mineral wandered, as chatoyancy, with light reflected from the inside, as it were, to the faceted surface. With the separation of external form from material substance, the mineral began to lose its magic aura, which was bound up with its material substance. The transition to the secular cult of beauty would soon dawn.

Light itself did not become the theme until it was technically possible to plan and repeat the making of regular facets in the working of gemstones, revolutionizing the way in which gemstones were handled. At the same time, faceting prepared the way for the mass deployment of jewellery stones in modern times by defining the brilliant-cut diamond as the prototype of the ›beautiful gemstone‹ and providing the bonus of a scientifically grounded description of how this could be done. What faceting gemstones, the creation of regular reflecting surfaces by using the laws of optics, entailed was, in terms of physics, the creation of a source of light that was virtual *qua* reflected and, therefore, transcendental. On the symbolic plane this corresponded to bringing together the divine principle and human reason in the aesthetic sense. The aural potential latent in this was even heightened by another circumstance: the hardness and coldness of the mineral, especially the diamond with its promise of eternity due to its hardness – properties, therefore, which removed this fire from the tactile onslaught of man and made the light all the more mysterious. By virtue of being remote from raptures that might be satisfied on the tactile plane, the emotional impact this light made on the plane of visual perception was multiplied. Further, banishing this supernatural looking light to an inaccessible-seeming mineral created an effect of placing the divine, as it were, in a tabernacle. In being virtual, it was also – to use the term that emerged in the Renaissance for what was not bound to any earthly place – utopian. Thus it prefigured Paradise, lost to man in the Fall yet regained by Christ's sacrifice. In the Christian iconography of Renaissance architecture and painting, the the columns of Solomon's Temple and the towers of the ›New Jerusalem‹ have bases of gemstones – in medieval thinking – and are represented as polygons. Symbolically speaking, however, the polygon as a form very often also stood for the body of the Virgin pregnant with the Son of God.

On the other hand, concomitantly with the introduction of the idea of reason as divinely induced, this era saw the secularisation of beauty, so often the subject of scholarly publications. In an attempt to achieve a reflection of the light shining on a stone that was as perfect as possible, faceting in an early form of brilliant cut assumed the guise of geometricizing formalism. When looked at in elevation from the side, the brilliant cut reveals an increasingly perfectionist striving to emphasize the decorative qualities of a stone. Its formal design still alluded to the unresolved mathematical problem of squaring the circle, thus justifying the meaning metaphorically assigned to it as the symbol of the transcendent, infinite divine. However, the use of the principles of numbers mysticism in faceting, the optical embedding of virtual light in the refulgent universe represented by the multiple refractions of light according to the by now secularised ideas of beauty now increasingly alluded to Freemasonry, the hermeticism of *manierismo* and the adaptation of the Islamic ornamental aesthetic in the Mediterranean.

Goldsmiths began – at first in Flanders and then throughout Europe – to smooth the surfaces of gemstones in the form of regular facets thanks to the invention of the horizontally turning cutting-wheel towards the close of the 15th century. Up to then the only cuts available to practitioners of gem-carving (the glyptic art) were the flat or table cut and the domed cabochon mentioned above. Faceting by rubbing was already known in India, the Near East and the Mediterranean in antiquity, albeit not in regular, symmetrically ordered surfaces.[18] The Renaissance ushered in ideas and ways of seeing which – in practical terms – made the surface of gemstones shine and ultimately, as faceting became increasingly sophisticated, lent them an aura that surpassed any natural phenomenon yet looked, of course, artificial.[19] The development of cutting also made possible the cutting of ever smaller (and cheaper) stones, thus creating the conditions under which mass production for a less affluent clientele might thrive.

The veneration of the aura of light in gemstones which had become divine through many individual steps was only feebly echoed in the profane cult of beauty prevail-

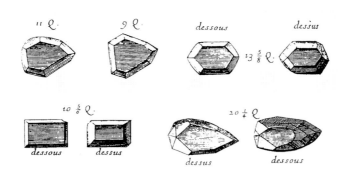

Verschiedene historische indische Diamanten in der Darstellung von Jean-Baptiste Tavernier, Mitte 17. Jh. ‖
Various historic Indian diamonds represented by Jean-Baptiste Tavernier, mid-17th century

dieses übernatürlich erscheinenden Lichts in ein unnahbar erscheinendes Mineral hatte zudem den Effekt einer Verortung des Göttlichen wie in einen Tabernakel. Als virtuelles Licht war es zugleich – verwendet man den in der Renaissance aufkommenden Begriff für das an keinen irdischen Ort Gebundene – utopisch. Es verwies damit auf das durch die Erbsünde verlorene irdische und das Selbstopfer Christi für die Menschen wiedergewonnene himmlische Paradies. Auch in der christlichen Ikonographie der Renaissancearchitektur und -malerei wurden die – im mittelalterlichen Denken – auf Edelsteinen begründeten Türme des Tempels Salomons und des »Neuen Jerusalem« polygonal dargestellt. Symbolisch stand diese Form allerdings auch sehr häufig für den Leib der den Gottessohn austragenden Maria.

Mit der Einführung der göttlich induzierten Vernunft vollzog sich andererseits in dieser Epoche gleichzeitig der von der Literatur häufig so bezeichnete Prozess der Säkularisierung des Schönen. Im Bestreben, eine möglichst vollkommene Reflexion des in den Stein einfallenden Lichts zu erzielen, gestaltete sich der Brillantschliff als geometrisierender Formalismus, der, betrachtet man ihn im Aufriss, zunehmend perfektionistischer die dekorativen Qualitäten der Steine in den Vordergrund stellte. Immer noch verwies die formale Gestaltung auf das nach wie vor ungelöste mathematische

Problem der Quadratur des Kreises und begründete so die metaphorische Sinnzuweisung als Symbol des transzendenten unendlichen Göttlichen. Aber: Die Anwendung zahlenmystischer Grundsätze bei der Facettierung, die optische Einbettung des virtuellen Lichts in die vielfach gebrochene schillernde Welt der Facetten nach den inzwischen säkular gewordenen Schönheitsvorstellungen bezogen sich in immer größerem Maße auf das Freimaurertum, den Hermetismus des *Manierismo* und auch auf die im Mittelmeerraum einsetzende Adaption der islamischen dekorativen Ästhetik.

Mit dem Glätten der Oberflächen von Edelsteinen in Form regelmäßig angelegter Facetten begannen die Goldschmiede – zunächst in Flandern und in Norditalien, dann auch im übrigen Europa – dank der Erfindung des horizontal drehenden Schleifrades gegen Ende des 15. Jahrhunderts. Bis dahin kannte man neben der Glyptik (Steinschneidekunst)

Diamant »Florentiner«, Indien, seit 1467 bekannt; Replikat von Rudolf Dröschel, Kristallmuseum Riedenburg/D ‖ Diamond ›Florentine‹, India, known since 1467; replica by Rudolf Dröschel, Kristallmuseum Riedenburg/D

ing in the modern age, to put it as Walter Benjamin did. Culminating in the brilliant cut, which exacted formalist perfectionism, the secular cult of beauty increasingly lacked the content on which the aura had been founded. Put another way: the absence of the divine became ever more palpable. This is especially true of the metaphor underlying faceting, which nowadays appears bereft of its former content.

BERND MUNSTEINER AND THE RENAISSANCE OF THE MINERAL

Still widespread in the Renaissance, sculpture and utilitarian objects made of crystals lost ground, becoming meaningless with the decline of the ruling houses of Europe, the transition to the age of mercantilism and the concomitant mass spread of jewellery. The *pietre dure* technique began to disappear and the art of gem-carving to decline. Only a few of the European gemstone workshops so numerous in the Renaissance – in Venice, Milan, Florence, Nuremberg, Prague, Fribourg, Paris, Bruges, to name just a few – now remain. Today only in the gemstone region of Idar-Oberstein are all techniques of working stones both by hand and industrially (from cutting to gem-carving and sculpture) still practised on a European scale and to European standards – and even there the trend is downwards.

The guild of gem-cutters had, however, already laid a stone in its path before it had even reached modern times. By tying themselves down to the brilliant cut as the sole universally valid ideal, gem-cutters left the domain of art to devote themselves forthwith to industrial manufacture and pay obeisance to the greater glory of the jewellery stone. Limitation to the normed ideal cut undermined creativity. It did bring enormous success in financial terms – on a worldwide scale – since the establishment of a norm in taste and technique also laid the groundwork for successful industrial production. It should be noted that, by Goethe's day, the art historical discourse engaged in by the German bourgeois chattering classes had consigned the goldsmith's craft – even that of a Benvenuto Cellini – to demimonde status in the art world.

At the end of the 1960s Bernd Munsteiner was the first to thaw the freeze which insistence on the brilliant cut had caused to set in. Replacing it with creative and artistic handling of minerals, he undertook to explore the art potential of the crystal. Utterly determined and revolutionary in his approach, he cast off the fetters of what had become a rigidly traditional craft by transferring as a student to the Pforzheim Hochschule für Gestaltung – although he had grown up and trained in a traditional Idar-Oberstein gem-cutting family. It is fascinating to see what he – from the standpoint of a contemporary artist –has made of the artistic dialogue with the mineral abandoned on the threshold of the modern age. This was to become a lifelong discourse, during which the artist not only thoroughly explored the aesthetic aspects of cutting. He also experimentally ›turned upside down‹ the traditionalist views of mineralogy on what crystals might allow in the way of free design.

In the early years Bernd Munsteiner discovered agate as his material of choice for reliefs. Since the early 1980s, on the other hand, he has used only transparent stones. Agate is the traditional stone of the gemstone region of Idar-Oberstein, to which he returned after finishing his studies. His exploration of agate also represented his

first questioning of the assumptions underlying crafts tradition of his native region. It was not long before he realised that agate was not very suitable as a material for sculpture, first, because it is not transparent and, second, because of its natural formation. The vivid markings on its surface in its natural state usually creates a highly pictorial effect, which duly shapes its aesthetic message. This stone did enable him to create hauntingly evocative and masterly reliefs (›Pictures‹ and jewellery) but not sculpture in the round. It took transparent minerals to open up an opportunity for him to come to grips as an artist with the dimension of space and its crystalline structure. He has always focused on both the mineral in its natural state and the quest for light and the traces left by light in stone.

REVITALISING SCULPTURE

Formally speaking, most of Bernd Munsteiner's work, on his own admission, links up with the tradition of gemstone sculpture which was predominant in the 18th century and on into the 19th alongside gem-cutting.[20]

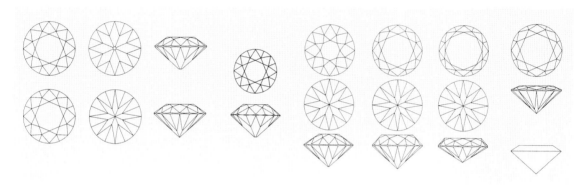

Verschiedene Diamantschliffe aus dem 20. Jahrhundert, nach Herbert Tillander ‖ Various 20th-century diamond cuts, from Herbert Tillander

den Treppenschliff sowie den schon erwähnten Rundschliff (Muggeln). Das Facettieren durch Reiben war zwar bereits in Indien, dem mittleren Orient und in der mediterranen Antike bekannt, allerdings nicht im Sinne der regelmäßigen, symmetrischen Anordnung der Facetten.[18] Mit der Renaissance tauchten die Ideen und Sichtweisen auf, die – gefasst in eine kunsthandwerkliche Sprache – die Oberfläche der Edelsteine zum Leuchten brachten und ihnen mit einer sich immer weiter verfeinerten Facettierung schließlich zu einer das Naturphänomen weit überstrahlenden, freilich artifiziellen Aura verhalfen.[19] Die Entwicklung der Schleiftechnik machte zudem das Schleifen immer kleinerer (und billigerer) Steine möglich und schuf dadurch die Voraussetzung zur Massenproduktion für den weniger finanzstarken bürgerlichen Kundenkreis.

Die Verehrung der in vielen Einzelschritten göttlich gewordenen Aura des Lichts im Edelstein fand, um es in der Sprache Walter Benjamins auszudrücken, im profanen Schönheitskult der Neuzeit nur ein nachklingendes Echo. Der im ebenso perfektionistischen wie formalistischen Brillantschliff kulminierende säkulare Schönheitskult entbehrt in zunehmendem Maße des die Aura begründenden Inhalts. Man könnte auch sagen: Die Abwesenheit des Göttlichen wird immer spürbarer. Für die inhaltsleer erscheinende Metaphorik des Facettschliffs der Gegenwart gilt dies in ganz besonderem Maße.

BERND MUNSTEINER UND DIE RENAISSANCE DES MINERALS

Die in der Renaissance noch verbreitete Skulptur und das Gebrauchsobjekt aus Kristallen waren mit dem Niedergang des europäischen Herrschaftsadels, dem Übergang in die bürgerliche Epoche und der damit einsetzenden massenhaften Verbreitung des Schmucks in ihrer Bedeutung zunehmend ins Hintertreffen geraten. Das Verschwinden beispielsweise der *Pietre dure*-Technik, die künstlerische Stagnation in der Glyptik und deren Niedergang setzten ein. Von der Vielzahl der europäischen Edelsteinmanufakturen der Renaissance – Venedig, Mailand, Florenz, Nürnberg, Prag, Freiburg, Paris, Brügge, um nur einige zu nennen – sind nur wenige erhalten geblieben. Heute werden im europäischen Maßstab lediglich in der Edelsteinregion Idar-Oberstein sämtliche handwerklichen und industriellen Bearbeitungstechniken (vom Schliff bis zur Glyptik und zur Skulptur) ausgeübt – allerdings auch dort mit abnehmender Tendenz.

Die Zunft der Edelsteinschleifer hatte sich vom Weg in die künstlerische Moderne jedoch bereits zu Beginn der Neuzeit selbst abgeschnitten: Mit der Festlegung auf den Brillantschliff als dem allein gültigen Ideal verabschiedeten sich die Schleifer aus der Kunst und widmeten sich fortan in industriellen Manufakturen der Pflege des säkularen Glanzes von Schmucksteinen. Die Festlegung auf den genormten Idealschliff unterminierte die Kreativität. Dieses allerdings – im Weltmaßstab betrachtet – mit sehr großem ökonomischen Erfolg, da die normierende Festlegung auf einen bestimmten Geschmack und eine bestimmte Technik zugleich auch die Voraussetzung einer erfolgreichen industriellen Produktion war. Anzumerken ist, dass bereits im kunsthistorischen Diskurs des Bildungsbürgertums der Goethe-Zeit die Goldschmiedearbeiten – sogar eines Benvenuto Cellini – wegen mangelnder Originalität dem Bereich der Halbkunst zugeordnet wurden.

Erst Bernd Munsteiner beginnt Ende der 60er Jahre des 20. Jahrhunderts, den durch die Fixierung auf den Brillantschliff eingetretenen Zustand der Erstarrung zugunsten eines

Sculpture, some of it on a considerable scale, worked from one piece of stone, is Munsteiner's chief domain. He has found his artistic voice in free sculpture. That is where he has experimentally developed – on the motto that the material provides an artist with what are infinite possibilities for design – revolutionary techniques of cutting and cuts, which he then adapts for use in his minuscule sculptures, reliefs and ›Pictures‹ cut on the reverse. By using transparent stones especially and working them in a particular way, he has opened up a spatial dimension within stones previously unimaginable in sculpture. This is an approach that is nothing short of revolutionary. His works are – except for two diamond cuts developed for serial production – one-off pieces. Munsteiner's work is entirely non-representational. However, the agates he has cut and the phallic-looking objects in the ›Symbolon‹ series are so provocative that they elicit free association or even psychoanalytical interpretation.

Munsteiner's first step, a momentous one, has been to free minerals from the chains of the market. He does not waste time on thinking about how he might enhance the market value of a stone by the way he works it. What matters to him is the configuration potential a stone has for art. His readiness to intervene massively in the material for art's sake, to remove large parts of the rough stone or to cut into it so deeply that it loses weight added insult to injury as far as the gemstone trade saw it during the early years of his career. After all, these policies questioned the assumptions of keeping the highest possible weight in carats as the standard by which market value is measured.

Since Munsteiner takes the natural formation of a stone as his point of departure in his art, he rejects out of hand the usual practice of demolishing a crystal into marketable shapes and sizes to milk the most money out of it (ill. p. 32). Munsteiner tries – against the conventional wisdom of the market – to keep a crystal as large as possible and as close to its original formation as he can and still work it. His sculptures defy easy access, often because of their breath-taking size. Viewers must first stop thinking in terms of carats, the usual quantifying standard of evaluation in the gemstone trade, before they address or be addressed by the message in the

Bernd Munsteiner, Bild »Landschaft«, 1986, Sarderonyxrelief, Silber (siehe auch S. 81) ||
Bernd Munsteiner, picture ›Landscape‹, 1986, sardonyx relief, silver (see also p. 81)

künstlerisch-kreativen Umgangs mit dem Mineral wieder aufzulösen und den Kristall aufs Neue als Werkstoff für die Kunst zu erschließen. Mit radikaler Entschlossenheit legt er – in der Tradition einer Idar-Obersteiner Schleiferfamilie aufgewachsen und ausgebildet – mit seinem Wechsel als Student an die Pforzheimer Hochschule für Gestaltung die Fesseln der erstarrten handwerklichen Tradition ab. Auf eine faszinierende Art und Weise nimmt er – aus dem Blickwinkel des zeitgenössischen Künstlers – die an der Schwelle zur Neuzeit eingestellte künstlerischen Auseinandersetzung mit dem Mineral wieder auf. Es sollte ein lebenslanger Diskurs werden, in dessen Verlauf sich der Künstler nicht nur mit den ästhetischen Fragen des Schliffs grundsätzlich auseinandersetzte, sondern auch die traditionellen Auffassungen der Mineralogie hinsichtlich einer freien Gestaltbarkeit von Kristallen experimentell »auf den Kopf« stellte.

Während Bernd Munsteiner in den ersten Jahren vor allem den Achat als künstlerischen Werkstoff für Reliefs entdeckte, verwendet er seit Beginn der 1980er Jahre ausschließlich transparente Steine. Die Auseinandersetzung mit dem Achat als dem Traditionsstein der Edelsteinregion Idar-Oberstein, in die er nach seiner Studienzeit zurückgekehrt war, ist zugleich die erste grundsätzliche Auseinandersetzung mit den handwerklichen Traditionen seiner Heimat. Schnell erkannte er allerdings, dass der Achat wegen seiner fehlenden Transparenz und vor allem wegen seines natürlichen Wuchses nur sehr eingeschränkt als plastisches Material tauglich ist: Die stark strukturierte Oberfläche des natürlichen Achats besitzt für sich betrachtet zumeist schon eine stark bildhafte Wirkung und ästhetische Botschaft. So ermöglichte der Stein ihm zwar die assoziative Schaffung von meisterhaften Reliefs (»Bilder« und Schmuck), nicht aber von Skulpturen. Nur das transparente Mineral eröffnete ihm die Chance der künstlerischen Auseinandersetzung mit der Dimension des Raumes an sich, aber auch die mit seiner kristallinen Struktur. Sein Interesse galt (und gilt) dabei sowohl dem natürlich gewachsenen Mineral als auch der Recherche nach dem Licht und den Spuren des Lichts im Stein.

DIE NEUBELEBUNG DER SKULPTUR

In formaler Hinsicht greift Bernd Munsteiner in den meisten seiner Arbeiten, auch nach eigenem Bekunden, die Tradition der bis ins 18./19. Jahrhundert neben dem Steinschnitt dominierenden Edelsteinskulptur wieder auf.[20] Aus einem Stein gearbeitete Skulpturen von zum Teil beträchtlicher Dimension machen Munsteiners Hauptwerk aus. In der freien Plastik sucht und findet er seine eigene künstlerische Sprache. Hier entwickelt er experimentell – nach der Devise, dass das Material dem Künstler zunächst einmal eine unendliche Vielzahl von Gestaltungsmöglichkeiten anbietet – neuartige Schleiftechniken und Schliffe, die er dann auch auf seine Kleinstplastiken, Reliefs und rückseitig

Bernd Munsteiner, Skulptur »Symbolon«, 1994, Bergkristall mit Rutil (siehe auch S. 138)
Bernd Munsteiner, sculpture ›Symbolon‹, 1994, rock crystal with rutile (see also p. 138)

material. Only once the obscuring veil of the market has been lifted can Munsteiner's works be interpreted in their natural context and given their proper place in cultural history.

And, finally, Munsteiner defies the ›dictates of purity‹ which has governed the valuation of minerals since antiquity, disqualifying as it does formations with inclusions as ›impure‹. The artist exposes this criterion, based on rarity, for what it is: market-orientated. He views purity as featurelessness or emptiness.

Rejecting the dictates of purity opens up possibilities for accessing what is each time a distinctively unique piece of natural mineral. For Munsteiner, it is the chatoyancy or inclusions in a rough stone which spark off his imagination, making each mineral a one-off gift of nature. With each stone he picks up, he starts off again on a quest, a scientific expedition departing from what is as a rule a rather unassuming rough stone for the inner structure of the crystal. Having rejected an aesthetic of the superficial which can be reproduced in multiples, he discovers new and different ›landscapes‹ in every stone while he

is tracking down the phenomenon of light in them, which never ceases to fascinate him. In this respect the artist is primarily concerned in many of his works (such as the works in agate, the ›Natural Movement‹ sequence or the ›Metamorphoses‹) with decoding the message inherent in the material and making it visible by the work he does to give it form. In thus addressing himself to the natural mineral formation, he opens up for himself and those who view his works an immediate and astonishing new approach to the microcosm of inorganic nature, thus also establishing the premises for an original work. His almost loving veneration for the natural material is what keeps him from working in a representational or – like hidebound representatives of the craft – even naturalistic vein. His terse comment on this is: ›A stone doesn't want to be a bird.‹

Bernd Munsteiner has acquired his specialist knowledge of mineralogy. He is a consummate mastery of his exacting craft and experienced in handling minerals. All this knowledge has not, however, hindered him in approaching stone with the aesthetic imagination of an artist. On the contrary, fulfilling these conditions is the only way to meet the requirements indispensable to discovering the latent potential for inherent form in such a seemingly archaic material and making it accessible to artistic endeavour. Without superb knowledge of the structure and often fraught tectonics of stones it would be hazardous, not to say impossible, to cut sculpture, especially fairly large-scale sculpture because the risk of breaks would be too great. As cosmopolitan as this artist is, his work should nonetheless be interpreted against the background of the gem-cutting tradition which thrives in Germany only in the gemstone region of Idar-Oberstein. Born into a gem-cutting family in the Hunsrück, Munsteiner has adopted an inward-directed stance towards the ritual of gemstone-cutting, which nowadays looks archaic indeed. His attitude to it alternates between close attention and stoic composure, virtues indispensable to his art. Immediately following his apprenticeship he left the bare Hunsrück, which was once an impoverished region, to take up his studies in Pforzheim. Yet he afterwards returned to the Hunsrück to find the inner peace he needed for his

work – embedded in a rural environment. An artist who at least ritually invokes the crafts tradition of gem-cutting, he has certainly maintained it within himself – by thinking about it – to a far greater extent than gem-cutting workshops which produce industrially could ever do. Munsteiner after all reflects in a meditative manner on cutting and the history of gem-cutting.

THE QUEST FOR THE AURA OF A STONE

This turn to sculpture in transparent minerals makes a preoccupation with space an ongoing theme in his work. Another is light, without which viewers could not glimpse the spatial dimension of the mineral. Munsteiner is well aware that this inner space in a crystal has one quality in particular for artist and viewer alike: it cannot be experienced in the tactile sense. Consequently, he only opens up in the light which follows the structure of the crystal – in two dimensions, as it were, as an image on the smooth surface of the object.
All work by Munsteiner, including his sculpture, has a distinctive face, i.e., a front and back defined – one

geschliffenen »Bilder« adaptiert. Insbesondere durch die Verwendung transparenter Steine und durch deren besondere Bearbeitung erschließt er in geradezu revolutionärer Weise die bis dahin in der Skulptur unvorstellbare räumliche Dimension im Inneren des Steins. Seine Arbeiten sind – mit Ausnahme von zwei für die Serienproduktion entwickelten Diamantschliffen – Unikate. Munsteiner arbeitet ausschließlich nicht-gegenständlich. Allerdings fordern beispielsweise die von ihm geschliffenen Achate oder die phallisch anmutenden Objekte der »Symbolon«-Reihe die freie Assoziation oder die tiefenpsychologische Deutung geradezu heraus.

Munsteiners erster und folgenreicher Schritt ist die sozusagen emanzipatorische Lösung der Mineralien aus den Fesseln einer marktmäßigen Wertbetrachtung. Er hält sich nicht mit der Frage auf, was er im pekuniären Sinne an Mehrwert aus einem Stein herausholen kann. Für ihn sind die künstlerischen Gestaltungspotenziale des Steines das Entscheidende. Seine Bereitschaft zu massiven Interventionen in das Material aus künstlerischen Gründen, zum Entfernen großer Teile des Rohsteins oder zu tiefen, Gewichtsverlust bewirkenden Einschnitten, waren in den ersten Jahren seines Schaffens für die Edelsteinbranche ein schwer zu ertragender Affront – stellten sie doch das Ziel der Erhaltung einer möglichst hohen Karatzahl als ökonomischen Bewertungsmaßstab prinzipiell in Frage.

Da Munsteiner sich auf den natürlichen Wuchs als Ausgangspunkt seiner künstlerischen Arbeit bezieht, weist er auch die branchenübliche Zertrümmerung des Kristalls unter ökonomischen Aspekten in marktgängige Formate zurück. Munsteiner versucht – wider die wirtschaftliche Ratio – den Kristall im größtmöglichen, noch bearbeitbaren Format zu erhalten (Abb. S. 32). Einem schnellen Zugang widersetzen sich seine Skulpturen schon wegen ihrer oft atemberaubende Dimensionierung. Der Betrachter muss zuerst das Denken in Karat, die gewohnten quantifizierenden Bewertungskriterien des Edelsteingeschäfts hinter sich lassen, bevor er sich der Botschaft des Materials zuwenden kann. Erst jenseits der verdunkelnden Folie des Marktes ist die Interpretation der Arbeiten Munsteiners in ihrem natur- und kulturhistorischen Kontext wirklich möglich.

Und schließlich widersetzt Munsteiner sich auch dem seit der Antike bei der Bewertung von Mineralien maßgeblichen Verdikt der »Reinheit« des Materials, welches den natürlichen, mit Einschlüssen versehenen Wuchs als »unrein« qualifiziert. Der Künstler entlarvt dieses auf der Seltenheit des Vorkommens basierende Kriterium als ausschließlich ökonomisch begründet. Er erkennt Reinheit als Merkmalslosigkeit oder Leere.

Die Zurückweisung des Reinheitsverdikts eröffnet ihm zugleich die Möglichkeit des Zugriffs auf ein jeweils unverwechselbares und einzigartiges Stück natürlichen Minerals. Für Munsteiner sind es gerade die changierenden farblichen Strukturen oder die vorgefundenen Einschlüsse im noch unbearbeiteten Stein, die zum Ausgangspunkt seiner Phantasie werden und jedes Mineral zu einem singulären Geschenk der Natur machen. Mit jedem Stein, den er in die Hand nimmt, macht er sich erneut auf die Suche, begibt sich vom Ausgangspunkt des äußerlich in der Regel sehr unscheinbaren Rohsteins auf eine Forschungsreise in das Innere der kristallinen Struktur. Mit seiner Absage an eine industriell multipel reproduzierbare Oberflächenästhetik entdeckt er in jedem Stein neue und andere abenteuerliche »Landschaften«, spürt dem für ihn immer wieder aufs Neue faszinierenden Phänomen des Lichts im Mineral nach. Insofern geht es dem Künstler bei vielen seiner Arbeiten (etwa seinen Achatarbeiten, der Werkfolge »Natural Movement« oder bei den »Metamorphosen«) vor allem darum, die jeweilige immanente Botschaft des Materials zu entschlüsseln und durch seine formgebenden Arbeit sichtbar zu machen. Die Hinwendung zum natürlich gewachsenen Mineral eröffnet ihm wie dem Betrachter seiner Werke einen unmittelbaren und überraschend neuen Zugang in den Mikrokosmos der anorganischen Natur und schafft so gleichzeitig die Voraussetzung zu einem originellen Werk. Die geradezu liebevolle Achtung vor dem natürlichen Material bewahrt ihn davor, gegenständlich oder – wie die Vertreter des Handwerks – gar naturalistisch zu arbeiten. Lakonisch meint er: »Ein Stein will kein Vogel sein.«

In einer eigenen Ausbildung erworbenes mineralogisches Fachwissen, handwerkliche Perfektion und Erfahrung im Umgang mit dem Mineral hindern Bernd Munsteiner nicht

might even say recorded – by the artist himself. The artist's objects follow a perspective ›suggested‹ to him by the material, the angle, as it were, from which they ›want‹ to be viewed and worked. The structure of a mineral, the emergence of inclusions or fractures, determine for the artist where the surface is on which the object will stand and the direction in which it will face. Engaging in a creative dialogue, Munsteiner follows the guideline established by his mineral, removes material to plot out the surface on which the object will stand as well as its back and front, focusing where he and others are to look by positioning cuts and laying out reflecting surfaces which are positive and negative in cut. His eye and his artistic invention follow the natural course of the material.

Munsteiner abandons his own entirely personal way of looking at and into the mineral, thus establishing guidelines to direct viewers' gaze. The observant eye is subtly led to and into the translucent and lucid sculpture – to the enigmatic enchantment of the mineral. It is also directed to Munsteiner's equally mysterious sleights of hand in cutting. In their genesis ›illusionist‹,

their mirroring reflections are virtually impossible for the unpractised eye of the beholder to grasp. Munsteiner is, however, not interested in effect *per se*. The artist's main preoccupation is – after having, for the time being, finished with agate and with the exception of the ›Symbolon‹ stones – with the problem of guiding the hexagonal crystal through the intervention effected by his cutting into a new, spectacular visual space. Munsteiner is concerned with transforming the image of the interior of the crystal, which appears through a planar cut and polished surface to be two-dimensional, into a structure that is perceived as three-dimensional. Following on a creative phase of ›reflecting [on] perspectives‹ in which he questioned the assumptions of mineralogy and proved experimentally, so to speak, the way crystalline materials lend themselves to free design, Munsteiner concentrated on developing special negative cuts, usually on the back face of a stone to create the spatial effects he wanted. For viewers, this is tantamount to a disturbing, dual sculptural quality, with the external sculptural form of the work related to viewers and their space, whereas the plasticity appearing in the interior of the object remains limited to the crystal and reflects the physical properties of its substance. Viewers experience this percept as a process, with their gaze literally being drawn into the crystal. A closer look reveals that sculptures, especially those done in transparent quartz since the 1990s, at first lose their three-dimensional quality with respect to their external proportions to become like pictures shining out from the interior of the crystal. However, even closer scrutiny reinstates a spatial dimension in yet another process of transformation – wrought by Munsteiner's magic.

The plasticity of Munsteiner's more recent sculpture – and his wall pictures really should be thus designated – is very difficult for the eye to grasp. It takes on plasticity in the disturbing interplay created by the optical transformation of the three-dimensional external form of the work into an inner plasticity that is in part reflected and only virtually visible. Thus Munsteiner's sculptures prove themselves to be both works with a sculptural quality and pictures. They are picture-like miniatures which lead into a natural landscape that has come to rest and radiates eternity but is – on the other hand, rhythmicised by

Munsteiner's cascading cuts and set in motion – once again transported to a virtual and ultimately also real third dimension.

In light, the inner space of the crystal reveals itself as a ›landscape‹. Concomitantly, it discloses the cipher for a subjective landscape of the psyche, one that is significant to cultural history. Not only can it be viewed in close connection with the emergence of gem-cutting on the threshold of the modern age in Europe. It is also linked with the evolution of our secularised notion of beauty. Since the age of humanism, radiant light has stood both for the conscious self in the sense of the ›enlightened self‹ and the divine principle visible in the world. The structure of the mineral crystal in which light is reflected signifies, in its regularity of form especially, the higher divine order. Landscape, on the other hand, especially the miniaturised nature in a mineral, has been available since the Renaissance as a surface on to which the psyche may project. This holds not only for the naturalistic reproduction of a landscape as found. The emotional loading created by projection is reinforced in the contemplation of miniature-like Arca-

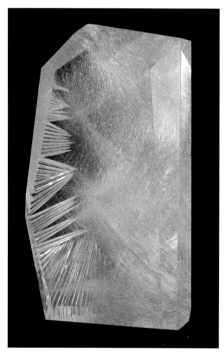

Bernd Munsteiner, Skulptur »Metamorphose I«, 1990, Bergkristall mit Rutil, Michael M. Scott Collection (siehe auch S. 100, 105) || Bernd Munsteiner, sculpture ›Metamorphosis I‹, 1990, rock crystal with rutile, Michael M. Scott Collection (see also pp. 100, 105)

daran, sich dem Stein ausschließlich mit dem ästhetischen Vorstellungsapparat des Künstlers zu nähern. Im Gegenteil: Sie sind sogar unabdingbare Voraussetzungen dafür, die jeweiligen verborgenen immanenten Gestaltungspotenziale des so archaisch anmutenden Materials zu entdecken und dieses für die künstlerische Arbeit zugänglich zu machen. Ohne hervorragende Kenntnisse über die Struktur und die oftmals spannungsvolle Tektonik der Steine wäre es sehr riskant und sogar unmöglich, insbesondere größere Skulpturen ohne Bruch zu schleifen. Bei aller Weltläufigkeit des Künstlers darf man sein Werk also durchaus auch vor dem Hintergrund der in Deutschland nur in der Edelsteinregion Idar-Oberstein lebendigen Schleifertradition interpretieren. Munsteiner, selbst Sohn einer Hunsrücker Edelsteinschleiferfamilie, hat mit dem heutzutage archaisch anmutenden Ritus des Steinschleifens jene innere Haltung zum Material gefunden, die in der Balance zwischen höchster Aufmerksamkeit und stoischer Gelassenheit für seine künstlerische Arbeit unerlässliche Tugend ist. Die karge, früher auch arme Welt des Hunsrücks hat er zwar nach seiner Lehre wegen des Studiums in Pforzheim schnell hinter sich gelassen. Doch kehrte er hernach wieder zurück, um – eingebettet in das ländliche Milieu – die innere Ruhe zur Arbeit zu finden. Als Künstler, der sich zumindest beim Ritual selbst auf die handwerklichen Traditionen des Edelsteilschliffs bezieht, hat er diese – indem er sich auf sie besinnt – gewiss in einem weit höheren Maße in sich bewahrt, als dies die industriell produzierenden Schleifereien vermögen. Nicht zuletzt reflektiert Munsteiner meditativ über das Schleifen und die Geschichte des Edelsteinschliffs.

DIE SUCHE NACH DER AURA DES STEINES

Mit seiner Hinwendung zur Skulptur aus transparentem Mineral wird nicht nur die Auseinandersetzung mit dem Raum zum fortwährenden Thema seiner Arbeit, sondern zugleich auch die mit dem Licht, das die räumliche Dimension des Minerals für den Betrachter erst sichtbar macht. Dabei ist Munsteiner sehr wohl bewusst, dass dieser innere Raum im Kristall für den Künstler wie für den Betrachter von einer besonderen Qualität ist: Haptisch nicht erfahrbar, erschließt er sich nur im Licht, das der kristallinen Struktur folgt – quasi zweidimensional, als Abbildung an der glatten Oberfläche des Objekts. Alle Arbeiten Munsteiners einschließlich seiner Skulpturen haben ein besonderes Gesicht, d.h. eine vom Künstler definierte – man könnte auch sagen: protokollierte – Vorder- und Rückseite. Seine Objekte folgen dabei zunächst einer vom Material dem Künstler quasi »suggestiv« vorgegebenen Perspektive, auf die hin sie betrachtet und auch bearbeitet werden »wollen«. Die mineralische Struktur, das Auftreten von Einschlüssen oder Bruchstellen bestimmen dem Künstler die Standfläche des Objekts und seine Ausrichtung. Im schöpferischen Dialog folgt Munsteiner der Vorgabe seines Minerals, legt durch Wegnahme von Material die Standfläche sowie die Vorder- und Rückseite des

Detail aus: Bernd Munsteiner, Skulptur »Metamorphose I«, 1990, Bergkristall mit Rutil, Michael M. Scott Collection (siehe auch S. 100, 105) || Detail: Bernd Munsteiner, sculpture »Metamorphosis I«, 1990, rock crystal with rutile, Michael M. Scott Collection (see also pp. 100, 105)

Bernd Munsteiner, Skulptur »Dom Pedro – Ondas Maritimas«, 1993, Aquamarin (siehe auch
S. 133) || Bernd Munsteiner, sculpture ›Dom Pedro – Waves of the Sea‹, 1993, aquamarine
(see also p. 133)

Objekts an, fokussiert den Blick durch das Setzen von Einschnitten, das Anlegen positiv
oder negativ geschliffener reflektierender Flächen. Sein Blick und seine künstlerischen
Interventionen folgen dem natürlichen Verlauf des Materials.

Munsteiner gibt seinen ganz persönlichen Blick auf und in das Mineral preis und macht
damit zugleich auch Vorgaben für die Blickrichtung des Betrachters. Das betrachtende
Auge wird subtil auf und zugleich in die luzide Skulptur geführt – hin zum geheimnis-
vollen Zauber des Minerals, aber auch zu den mindestens ebenso geheimnisumwitterten
schleiferischen Kunststücken Munsteiners, deren spiegelnde Reflexe in ihrer Genese
nicht nur für den ungeübten Betrachter »illusionistisch« und kaum nachzuvollziehen
sind. Allerdings geht es Munsteiner nicht um den Effekt an sich: Der Künstler setzt sich –
nach dem vorläufigen Abschluss seiner Beschäftigung mit dem Achat und mit einer
Ausnahme bei den »Symbolon«-Steinen – hauptsächlich mit der Problemstellung
auseinander, den hexagonalen Kristall durch seine schleiferische Intervention in einen
neuen, spektakulären Sehraum zu überführen. Munsteiners Anliegen ist, das durch eine
plan geschliffene und polierte Oberfläche zweidimensional erscheinende Bild des Kristall-
inneren in eine als dreidimensional wahrgenommene Struktur zu transformieren.

Nach der für sein Werk grundlegenden Schaffensphase der »Reflektierenden Perspektiven«,
in der er entgegen der Annahme der Mineralogie quasi experimentell die freie Gestaltbarkeit kristalliner Materialien nachwies, konzentrierte sich Munsteiner auf die
Entwicklung spezieller negativer, zumeist von der Rückseite des Steines her eingebrachter
Schliffe, um die gewünschten Raumeffekte zu erzielen. Für den Betrachter kommt es zu
einer irritierenden doppelten Plastizität des Werks, bei der die äußere plastische Form
sich auf den Betrachter und seinen Raum bezieht, während die im Inneren des Objekts
erscheinende Plastizität auf den Kristall beschränkt bleibt und seine Materialität abbildet.
Für den Betrachter stellt sich diese Wahrnehmung als ein Prozess dar, bei dem sein
Blick förmlich in den Kristall hineingezogen wird: Bei näherem Hinsehen verlieren
insbesondere die seit den 1990er Jahren entstandenen Skulpturen aus transparenten
Quarzen zunächst ihre Dreidimensionalität im Hinblick auf ihre äußeren Proportionen.

Sie werden gleichsam zu aus dem Inneren des Kristalls heraus scheinenden Bildern. Bei nochmals näherem Hinsehen aber erhalten sie in einem weiteren Transformationsprozess – Munsteiners Zauberwerk – wiederum eine räumliche Dimension.

Die mit den Augen nur schwer zu fassende Plastizität der späteren Munsteiner-Skulpturen – und eigentlich muß man auch seine Wandbilder als solche bezeichnen – stellt sich durch das irritierende Wechselspiel ein, das bei der optischen Transformation der dreidimensionalen äußeren Gestalt des Werks in eine zum Teil nur gespiegelt-virtuell sichtbare, innere Dreidimensionalität zustande kommt. Munsteiners Plastiken erweisen sich dabei als plastische Werke und Bilder zugleich: bildhafte Miniaturen, die in eine versteinerte, zur Ruhe gekommene und Ewigkeit ausstrahlende Naturlandschaft hineinführen, die aber – auf der anderen Seite durch Munsteinersche Schliffkaskaden rhythmisiert und in Bewegung gebracht – wieder in eine virtuelle und schließlich auch reale Dreidimensionalität überführt werden.

Im Licht zeigt sich der innere Raum des Kristalls als eine »Landschaft«. Es erscheint damit zugleich auch die kulturhistorisch bedeutsame Chiffre der subjektiven Seelenlandschaft, die nicht nur in einem engen Zusammenhang mit der Entstehung der Edelsteinschleiferei an der Schwelle der europäischen Neuzeit gesehen werden kann, sondern die auch mit der Entwicklung unserer säkularisierten Vorstellung von der Schönheit verbunden ist. Das strahlende Licht steht seit dem Zeitalter des Humanismus sowohl für das erkennende Ich im Sinne eines »erleuchteten Ich« als auch für das in der Welt sichtbare göttliche Prinzip. Die kristalline Struktur des Minerals, in der sich das Licht spiegelt, verweist insbesondere in ihrer Regelmäßigkeit auf die höhere göttliche Ordnung. Landschaft hingegen, insbesondere auch die im Mineral miniaturisierte Natur, steht seit der Renaissance als Projektionsflächen der Psyche zur Verfügung. Dieses gilt nicht nur für die naturalistische Abbildung einer vorgefundenen Landschaft. Die projektive emotionale Aufladung verstärkt sich bei der Betrachtung miniaturhafter arkadischer Landschaften – die bis ins 20. Jahrhundert hinein gepflegte »schöne Idylle« –, die sich beispielsweise beim glatten Anschliff von Achaten zeigen. Der Blick in das Innere des Kristalls wendet sich stets zu

dian landscapes – the ›idyllic beauty‹ cultivated on into the 20th century – which are revealed, for instance, when agates are flat-cut into plaques. The glimpse of the interior of the crystal invariably changes into an insight into one's own psyche, one that mobilizes both wanderlust and yearnings for closeness, sparking off the romantic malaise mirrored in those landscape microcosms and reflecting will-o'-the-wisps within the crystal.

Recurring to this cipher for the landscape of the psyche, Munsteiner sticks with it in his work for long stretches. In particular, his rejection of traditional cutting, which aims solely at creating the effect of ›brilliance‹ by means of the most perfect possible reflection of light shining on the stone, is what keeps his eyes open for the inner workings of the natural mineral formation. Munsteiner's meticulously and strikingly placed cuts create the setting for such mineral landscapes. The reflections and light effects thus elicited guide towards, instead of away from, the material. They neither stage the transcendental divine light as in the late Middle Ages and the Renaissance nor represent secular symbols of the cult of beauty as such.

Munsteiner's art enables all viewers to have subjective access to the stone and opens up to them the possibility of mirroring their own psyches. Even though he deploys the themes and techniques traditional to the craft of working minerals, his works abolish conventional notions of what the formal guise of beauty must be, thus making all viewers receptive to a modern yet entirely personal experience of art. Munsteiner's works are, therefore, given their aura through viewers' subjective experience of art. In letting themselves in for a work, deciphering it and at the same time mirroring themselves in it, they recreate it – by ideation.

The view which Munsteiner opens up into the universe of the crystal reveals inorganic nature of a beauty from which eternity emanates, that is at first remote from the known features of life and transience. The crystal radiating eternity, however, conceals the inherent dimension of time because it negates all chronicity: sheer provocation in a world that measures time by seconds. On the one hand, Bernd Munsteiner underscores the frozen beauty of the imperishable crystal as something beautiful found in nature, albeit remote from life, if not downright

Detail aus: Bernd Munsteiner, »Reflektierende Perspektiven«, 1992, Turmalin, Michael M. Scott Collection (siehe auch S. 115) ‖ Detail: Bernd Munsteiner, ›Reflecting Perspectives‹, 1992, tourmaline, Michael M. Scott Collection (see also p. 115)

einem Blick in das Innere der eigenen Psyche, mobilisiert Fernweh wie Sehnsucht nach Nähe, wird zum Auslöser jener romantischen Krankheit, die sich in den mikrokosmischen Landschaften und reflektierenden Irrlichtern im Kristall spiegelt.

Dieser Chiffre für die Seelenlandschaft wendet sich Munsteiner über weite Strecken seines Schaffens immer wieder zu. Insbesondere seine Abwendung vom traditionellen Schliff, der ausschließlich auf den Effekt der »Brillanz« durch eine möglichst vollkommene Reflexion des in den Stein einfallenden Lichts abzielt, gibt erst den Blick frei in das Innere des natürlich gewachsenen Minerals. Munsteiners sorgfältig und effektvoll gesetzten Schliffe dienen dabei der Inszenierung dieser mineralischen Landschaft. Die dadurch entstehenden Reflexionen und Lichteffekte führen zum Material und nicht von ihm weg. Sie sind weder, wie im ausgehenden Mittelalter oder in der Renaissance, Inszenierungen eines transzendentalen göttlichen Lichts noch als deren säkulares Sinnbild ein Kult des Schönen an sich.

Munsteiner Kunst ermöglicht jedem Betrachter einen subjektiven Zugang zum Stein und eröffnet ihm hierdurch wiederum die Möglichkeit der Spiegelung der eigenen Psyche. Munsteiners Arbeiten lösen, obwohl sie die Themen und Techniken der traditionellen Mineralbearbeitung aufnehmen, die habituellen Vorstellungen von der formalen Gestalt des Schönen völlig auf und machen so den Weg frei für ein modernes, ganz persönliches Kunsterlebnis eines jeden Betrachters. Die eigentliche Auratisierung des Munsteiner-Werks erfolgt so mit dem subjektiven Kunsterlebnis des Betrachters, der, indem er sich auf das Werk einlässt, es dechiffriert und zugleich auch sich selbst in ihm reflektiert, es erneut – ideell – erstehen lässt.

Der Blick, den Munsteiner in die Welt des Kristalls eröffnet, zeigt eine anorganische Natur von einer Ewigkeit ausstrahlenden Schönheit, der die bekannten Merkmale des Lebens und der Vergänglichkeit zunächst sehr fremd ist. Der Ewigkeit ausstrahlende Kristall birgt aber immanent die Dimension der Zeit, indem er jede Zeitlichkeit negiert: die reine Provokation in einer Welt, die ihre Zeit im Sekundentakt misst. Bernd Munsteiner stellt auf der einen Seite die gefrorene Schönheit des unvergänglichen Kristalls als ein lebensfernes, wenn nicht –feindliches, vorfindliches Naturschöne heraus (laut Plinius d. Ä. hielt man in der Antike den Bergkristall für versteinertes Eis), das auf der anderen Seite erst durch das Schleifwerk des Künstlers in eine natürliche Bewegung, ja sogar in einen reflektierend flimmernden Rhythmus gewiegt wird und als so beseeltes Kunstwerk die Aussöhnung des Menschen mit der kalten Natur betreiben kann. Es ist das Werk des Künstlers, das die mineralische Natur mit ihrem poetischen Lebenshauch durchzieht und den Kristall für den Betrachter nahbar macht und gewissermaßen »erdet«. Es ist die lebendige Aura des schönen Kunstwerks, die den Betrachter über seinen Schmerz in der Erfahrung des unbeseelten Minerals – Symbol einer von Gott verlassenen Welt – tröstet und ihm Hoffnung verheißt. Das ewig schöne Werk des Künstlers im Kristall symbolisiert die irdischen Paradiese und dessen Freuden. Munsteiners Arbeiten betreiben unter diesem Aspekt einen ausgesprochenen Kult des Schönen, der es letzten Endes naheliegend

Detail aus: Bernd Munsteiner, Skulptur »Metamorphose II«, 1990, Bergkristall mit Rutil (siehe auch S. 107) || Detail: Bernd Munsteiner, sculpture ›Metamorphosis II‹, 1990, rock crystal with rutile (see also p. 107)

inimical to it (according to Pliny the Elder, Greco-Roman antiquity thought rock crystal was petrified ice). On the other hand, only the artist's cutting can set this beauty in natural motion, let alone rock it in a reflecting, flickering rhythm so that it, *qua* animate work of art, can inaugurate the reconciliation of man with bleak nature. It is the artist's work which quickens mineral nature with this poetic breath of life by making the crystal accessible to viewers and, in a certain sense, ›earthing‹ it. It is the quickened aura of the beautiful work of art which consoles viewers for the pain they feel in experiencing the soullessness of the mineral – symbolizing a world abandoned by God – and gives them hope. The eternally beautiful work by the artist in crystal symbolizes the earthly paradise and its delights. Viewed in this light, Munsteiner's works unabashedly pay tribute to a cult of beauty. Further, following up this line of thinking to its logical conclusion would imply wearing his objects as body jewellery. Munsteiner's stones, however, always develop a life of their own informed as they are by a forceful dynamic which elevates them above a plane of existence where they would be merely appendages to jewellery.

With each work the artist – fully observant of the mineralogical, that is, scientific approach – embarks on a fresh quest for the essence, the spiritual substance of the crystal which shines out to him from within the stone, its unique and distinctive material properties, which seem to inhere in it like an ephemeral ghost from a pantheistically inspirited nature. Bernd Munsteiner tries to grasp the spirit of the crystal and to render it artistically as poetry cut in visual terms. In so doing he leads the viewer's eye into the material structure of the crystal while at the same time placing, through his work, the substance of the crystal on a symbolic plane. At this point the affinities of his work with the conception of nature entertained in the Romantic period clearly emerge. Many of these works might, of course, be read like a diorama of the dramatic changes in light incurred in images of night and day. On the other hand, however, they must also be grasped as contemporary icons of nature eternally transcending time.

As we have already seen, gem-cutting, as Bernd Munsteiner practises the art, first of all places the physical properties of the mineral at the centre of the work and shows them, literally – if you want to put it that way – to the viewer. The aura split off the material by faceting returns to dwell in the crystal. It does so, however, not to persist there as something naturally beautiful but to be immediately elevated by the artist to the symbolic plane. Yet Munsteiner, on the other hand, synchronously subverts the physical properties of the material by presenting them as ideal artistically configured reflection – in the literal sense of the term as well – as a work of art.

Occasionally there arises in Munsteiner's work a brief flash of wit and intellectual interplay between the dimensions, between what is art and what is natural, between the reality and the virtual, between appearances and stone. However, through his works wafts a deeper seriousness, confessing to awe of the material, not unlike the awe experienced before the sublime. Indeed, Munsteiner's artistic encounter with a crystal, once he has left behind him the sphere of superficial aesthetics and the aesthetic of surfaces, inevitably leads him back to the meaningful plane of the sublime as it was waiting to be found in the medieval aura of the beautiful stone symbolizing God.

Bernd Munsteiner has striven as no other artist has to find and keep finding, original solutions for the theme of light in stone above and beyond what is to him the reiterative iconography devoid of content as ritualised by the industrial production of gemstones for jewellery. As he sees it, establishing the brilliant cut as the arbiter of taste represented not only the onset of a protracted process of creative impoverishment in the handling of minerals. He realised, rightly, that reduction of design to cut for the sake of a glittering reflecting surface was also linked with the loss of the physical substance of the material – and, therefore, inevitably, the loss of its natural charm. Munsteiner wants to rediscover the aura of the stone that has faded in the ritual of cutting.[21] As a result, his work might be termed the resumption of the quest for the aura of beauty in stone. In a sense, what is at stake for him is discovering the quintessential aesthetic in each material and to work it through as spiri-

erscheinen lassen muss, seine Objekte auch als Körperschmuck zu tragen. Munsteiners Steine entwickeln dabei allerdings stets durch ihre kraftvolle Dynamik ein Eigenleben, das sie über eine Existenz als bloßer Annex eines Schmucks hinaus hebt.

Der Künstler begibt sich – bei aller mineralogisch-naturwissenschaftlichen Herangehensweise – mit einem Werk jedes Mal erneut auf die Suche nach dem Wesen, der spirituellen Substanz des Kristalls, die für ihn aus dem Inneren des Steins heraus zu scheinen, seiner jeweils einzigartigen Materialität wie ein ephemerer Geist aus einer pantheistisch beseelten Natur anzuhaften scheint. Bernd Munsteiner sucht diesen Geist des Kristalls zu erfassen und ihn künstlerisch als geschliffene Poesie für den Betrachter sichtbar darzustellen. Er führt den Blick des Betrachters in die materielle Struktur des Kristalls hinein und stellt durch sein Werk gleichzeitig die Substanz des Kristalls auf der Symbolebene dar. An diesem Punkte tritt die Affinität dieses Werks zur Naturkonzeption der Romantik deutlich hervor. Viele der Arbeiten können zwar sicherlich wie ein Diorama im dramatischen Lichtwechsel als Tag-Nacht-Bild gelesen werden. Andererseits sind sie aber auch als zeitgenössische Ikonen einer über die Dimension der Zeit erhabenen ewigen Natur zu verstehen.

Bernd Munsteiners Schleifkunst stellt, wie weiter oben dargestellt, einerseits zunächst die Materialität des Minerals in den Mittelpunkt des Werks und führt diese – wenn man so will – bildhaft dem Betrachter vor Augen. Die mit dem Facettenschliff vom Material abgespaltene Aura kehrt wieder in den Kristall zurück. Allerdings nicht um dort als Naturschönes zu verharren, sondern um vom Künstler umgehend auf die Symbolebene gehoben zu werden. Doch Munsteiner hebt andererseits und gleichzeitig eben diese Materialität des Materials auch wieder auf, indem er sie als ideelle, künstlerisch gestaltete Reflexion – auch im Wortsinne –, als Kunstwerk eben, präsentiert. Zwar stellt sich in Munsteiners Werk häufig auch ein kurzweiliges, gelegentlich witziges und intellektuelles Wechselspiel zwischen den Dimensionen, zwischen Kunsthaftem und Naturhaftem, zwischen Realität und Virtuellem, zwischen Schein und Stein ein. Aber durch seine Arbeiten weht ein tiefer, Ehrfurcht vor dem Material bekennender Ernst, der nicht unähnlich ist der ehrfürchtigen Haltung vor dem Erhabenen. In der Tat führt auch Munsteiners künstlerische Begegnung mit dem Kristall, nachdem er die Sphäre der Oberflächenästhetik hinter sich gelassen hat, zwangsläufig in diese sinnstiftende Dimension des Erhabenen, wie sie in der mittelalterlichen Aura des Gott symbolisierenden schönen Steins noch vorzufinden war, zurück.

Wie kein anderer hat Bernd Munsteiner versucht, für das Thema Licht im Stein immer wieder originale Antworten jenseits der für ihn zur inhaltsleeren, von der industriellen Schmucksteinproduktion ritualisiert wiederholten Ikonographie zu finden. In seinem Empfinden war die den Geschmack prägende Festlegung auf den Brillantschliff nicht nur der Anfang eines lange anhaltenden Prozesses der schöpferischen Verarmung im Umgang mit dem Mineral. Zurecht hat er erkannt, dass mit der Reduzierung der Gestaltung auf den Schliff einer brillierend reflektierenden Oberfläche auch der Verlust der Materialität des Minerals – und damit zwangsläufig auch der seines natürlichen Reizes – verbunden ist. Munsteiner will die im schleiferischen Ritual verblasste Aura des Steines neu entdecken.[21] Seine Arbeit könnte man somit als die Wiederaufnahme der Recherche nach der Aura des Schönen im Stein bezeichnen. Es geht ihm gewissermaßen darum, im Material die jeweilige ästhetische Substanz für sich zu entdecken und diese als geistigen Gehalt für den Betrachter herauszuarbeiten. Der oben vollzogene Rekurs auf die Verwendung der Mineralien in der europäischen Kulturgeschichte führt dabei auch zu Munsteiners künstlerischem Ansatz. Was die Verwendung des Rohstoffs Mineral betrifft, hat Munsteiner allerdings den Kult des Schönen gleichzeitig sowohl aus der Fessel der theologischen Kosmologie des endenden Mittelalters als auch aus der mit dem Brillantschliff in der Renaissance entstandenen Warenästhetik befreit. Damit erst war der Weg für eine zeitgenössische künstlerische Auseinandersetzung mit dem Material und den aus ihm resultierenden Gestaltungsmöglichkeiten eröffnet.

Bernd Munsteiner, Skulptur »Rhythmus I«, 1994, Aquamarin, Platin, Michael M. Scott Collection (siehe auch S. 148) || Bernd Munsteiner, sculpture ›Rhythm I‹, 1994, aquamarine, platinum, Michael M. Scott Collection (see also p. 148)

tual and intellectual content for the viewer. The discussion at the beginning on the use of minerals in European cultural history has led into Munsteiner's approach to his art. As for the use of mineral as his material of choice, Munsteiner has, however, liberated the cult of the beautiful from the chains of late medieval theological cosmology. He has also freed it from the constraints of the consumer aesthetic which grew out of the Renaissance to culminate in the brilliant cut. This is what has paved the way for a contemporary artistic dialogue with the material and the design potential ensuing from it.

With his work, Munsteiner led sculpture in gemstones to the aesthetic debates raging in the 20th century, without negating the archaic strata in humanity's relationship with stone and precious stones in particular. Munsteiner's gemstone sculptures evade *eo ipso* the prevailing culture of representation aimed at performative eventfulness as well as transient reception. On the other hand, they tower – despite their relatively small spatial extension – over our fleeting lifetime as monumental symbols of eternity.

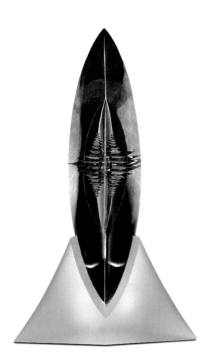

Bernd Munsteiner, Skulptur »Impressionen«, 1988, Rauchquarz, Bergkristall, Silber, Michael M. Scott Collection (siehe auch S. 96) || Bernd Munsteiner, sculpture ›Impressions‹, 1988, smoky quartz, rock crystal, silver, Michael M. Scott Collection (see also p. 96)

Munsteiner führt mit seinem Werk die Edelsteinskulptur an die künstlerischen Debatten des 20. Jahrhunderts heran, ohne die archaischen Schichten in der Beziehung des Menschen zum Stein und zum Edelstein im Besonderen zu negieren. Munsteiners Edelsteinskulpturen entziehen sich *eo ipso* sowohl einer auf performative Ereignishaftigkeit ausgerichteten Darstellungskultur als auch der Rezeption im Vorbeigehen. Andererseits ragen sie – trotz ihrer relativ geringen räumliches Ausdehnung – als monumentale Symbole des Ewigen in unsere flüchtige Lebenszeit hinein.

[1] Aus dem Gedicht »Trunkes Lied«, in: Friedrich Nietzsche, Also sprach Zarathustra, in: Werke in drei Bänden, Band 2, München 1994, S. 558.

[2] Bernd Munsteiner hält den Begriff »Edelstein« prinzipiell für problematisch und spricht im Bezug auf seinen Werkstoff lieber von »Mineral« oder »Stein«. Der Autor verwendet den Begriff aus Gründen der Lesbarkeit des Textes gelegentlich trotzdem.

[3] Faszination Edelstein. Aus den Schatzkammern der Welt. Mythos. Kunst. Wissenschaft, Ausstellungskatalog Hessisches Landesmuseum Darmstadt, Darmstadt 1992.

[4] Karl-Heinz Kohl, Die Magie der Dinge. Geschichte der sakralen Objekte; München 2003. Zur Herstellung und Verwendung von magischen Gemmen in der Spätantike vgl. Simone Michel, Bunte Steine – Dunkle Bilder: »Magische Gemmen«, Hamburg 2001.

5 Plinius, Naturkunde XXXVII, Zürich 1994.

6 In diesem Zusammenhang ist besonders seine ausführliche Beschreibung der Provenienzen der Edelsteine und des bis nach Ost- und Südostasien reichenden Fernhandels bemerkenswert. Plinius, Naturkunde XXXVII, Zürich 1994.

7 Zu den »Wölkchen« im Smaragd siehe Plinius, a.a.O., S. 57, zu den »Wölkchen« im Beryll siehe S. 63.

8 Theo Jülich, Zur Verwendung von Edelsteinen im Mittelalter, in: Faszination Edelstein, a.a.O. (Anm. 3), S. 64.

9 Martina Harms, Edelsteine in der Antike, in: Faszination Edelstein, a.a.O. (Anm. 3), S. 59.

10 Vgl. hierzu: Theo Jülich, a.a.O., S. 60–69, sowie: Hans Hahnloser, Susanne Brugger-Koch, Corpus der Hartsteinschliffe des 12.–15. Jahrhunderts, Berlin 1985.

11 Theo Jülich, a.a.O., S. 60.

12 Karl-Heinz Kohl interpretiert das Reliquiar als die anorganische Substanz der Reliquie. Vgl.: Karl-Heinz Kohl., a.a.O. (Anm. 4), S. 57 f.

13 Zur moralisch-allegorischen Steininterpretation des Mittelalters: Hans Hahnloser, Susanne Brugger-Koch, a.a.O. (Anm. 10), S. 6–12.

14 Theophil Spoerri, Dante und die europäische Literatur, Stuttgart 1963, S. 43. Zusätze in eckigen Klammern von W. L.

15 Vgl. hierzu. das Kapitel »Die symbolische Sprache der Architektur« in: Jörg Träger, Renaissance und Religion, München 1987, S. 327 ff.

16 Vgl. hierzu beispielsweise die Darstellung des Polyeders in Albrecht Dürers Tugendbild »Melancholia I«.

17 Marsilio Ficino, Traktate zur platonischen Theologie, Berlin 1993, S. 137 f.

18 Vgl. hierzu: Jean Baptiste Tavernier, Reisen zu den Reichtümern Indiens. Abenteuerliche Jahre beim Großmogul 1641–1667, Stuttgart, Wien, Bern 1984, S. 190.

19 Zum Prozess der Entwicklung des Brillantschliffs siehe besonders: Herbert Tillander, Diamond Cuts in Historic Jewellery 1381–1910, London 1995.

20 Seine Werke entstehen sämtlich als zunächst zweckfreie Arbeiten, auch wenn sie zu einem nicht unerheblichen Teil zu einem späteren Zeitpunkt – und heute üblicherweise von der Hand anderer – die Funktionszuweisung als Schmucksteine bekommen.

21 Dabei hat er die auf eine optimale Material- und Lichtausnutzung ausgerichtete Perfektion des Brillantschliffs durchaus auch als Herausforderung gesehen und in technischer Hinsicht keineswegs vor ihr kapituliert wie etwa der von ihm für die Industrie entwickelte »Spirit«- oder »Context«- Schliff zeigt.

1 From the poem ›Trunkes Lied‹, in: Friedrich Nietzsche, Also sprach Zarathustra, in: Werke in drei Bänden, Vol. 2, Munich 1994, p. 558.

2 Bernd Munsteiner regards the term ›gemstone‹ as problematic on principle and prefers to speak of the material he works with as ›mineral‹ or ›stone‹. The author nevertheless uses the term for readability's sake.

3 Faszination Edelstein. Aus den Schatzkammern der Welt. Mythos. Kunst. Wissenschaft, exhib. cat. Hessisches Landesmuseum Darmstadt, Darmstadt 1992.

4 Karl-Heinz Kohl, Die Magie der Dinge. Geschichte der sakralen Objekte; Munich 2003. On the making and use of magical gems in late antiquity cf Simone Michel, ›Bunte Steine – Dunkle Bilder: ›Magische Gemmen‹, Hamburg 2001.

5 Pliny the Elder, Naturkunde [Naturalis Historia] XXXVII, Zurich 1994.

6 In this connection his extensive descriptions of the provenance of gems and the trade routes extending as far as East and South-East Asia are particularly remarkable. Pliny, Naturalis Historia XXXVII, Zurich 1994.

7 On the ›little clouds‹ in the emerald see Pliny the Elder, loc. cit., p. 57; on the ›little clouds‹ in beryl see p. 63.

8 Theo Jülich, Zur Verwendung von Edelsteinen im Mittelalter, in: Faszination Edelstein, loc. cit. (n. 3), p. 64.

9 Martina Harms, Edelsteine in der Antike, in: Faszination Edelstein, loc. cit. (n. 3), p. 59.

10 Cf on this: Theo Jülich, loc. cit., pp. 60–69, and: Hans Hahnloser, Susanne Brugger-Koch, Corpus der Hartsteinschliffe des 12.–15. Jahrhunderts, Berlin 1985.

11 Theo Jülich, loc. cit., p. 60.

12 Karl-Heinz Kohl interprets reliquary as the inorganic substance of the relic. Cf: Karl-Heinz Kohl., loc. cit. (n. 4), p. 57f.

13 On the moral and allegorical interpretation of stone in the Middle Ages: Hans Hahnloser, Susanne Brugger-Koch, loc. cit. (n. 10), pp. 6–12.

14 Theophil Spoerri, Dante und die europäische Literatur, Stuttgart 1963, p. 43. Additional remarks in brackets by W. L.

15 Cf on this the chapter ›Die symbolische Sprache der Architektur‹ in: Jörg Träger, Renaissance und Religion, Munich 1987, p. 327f.

16 Cf on this, for instance, the representation of a polyhedron in Albrecht Dürer's virtue picture ›Melencolia I‹.

17 Marsilio Ficino, Traktate zur platonischen Theologie, Berlin 1993, p. 137f.

18 Cf on this: Jean Baptiste Tavernier, Reisen zu den Reichtümern Indiens. Abenteuerliche Jahre beim Großmogul 1641–1667, Stuttgart, Vienna, Bern 1984, p. 190.

19 On the process of developing diamond cuts, see especially: Herbert Tillander, Diamond Cuts in Historic Jewellery 1381–1910, London 1995.

20 All his works are created without a purpose, even though quite a few of them are later – and nowadays usually by other hands – assigned the function of stones in jewellery.

21 He has also certainly viewed the perfection of the brilliant cut, which aims at optimal exploitation of both the material and light, as a challenge and he has not capitulated to it in terms of technique, as the ›Spirit‹ and ›Context‹ cuts he has designed for industry show.

WERKGRUPPEN

GROUPS OF WORKS

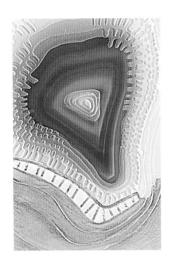

ACHATRELIEFS

Das unablässig wechselnde Spiel der Farben und Formen des Achats regt zu phantasievollen Miniaturlandschaften und grafisch gestalteten Reliefs an: Projektionsflächen des Psychischen. Die Auseinandersetzung mit dem Traditionsstein der Väter steht bei Bernd Munsteiners Arbeiten am Anfang.

AGATE RELIEFS

The perpetual play of colour and form in agate inspires imaginative miniature landscapes and graphically configured reliefs: surfaces on to which the psyche can project. His preoccupation with the traditional stone his father worked with stands at the beginning of Bernd Munsteiner's work.

REFLEKTIERENDE PERSPEKTIVEN

Luzide Kristalle wie Turmalin, Amethyst oder Aquamarin stimulieren Bernd Munsteiner zur freien Plastik. Transparenz und Reflexion des Lichts sind die Basis der anhaltenden künstlerischen Recherche nach den inneren und äußeren Sehräumen, nach immer neuen – dem Betrachter illusionistischen oder spektakulären – Blicken auf und in das Mineral.

REFLECTING PERSPECTIVES

Translucent crystals such as tourmaline, amethyst and aquamarine stimulate Bernd Munsteiner to create free sculpture. Transparency and reflecting light are the basis for the ongoing artistic quest for the inner and outer visual spaces, for new views each time – to the viewer illusionist or spectacular – of and into the mineral.

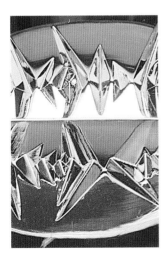

INSIDE SELECTING

Eine oder mehrere markante, symmetrisch entlang einer Längsachse verlaufende Einkerbungen signalisieren: das weibliche Geschlecht. Verspielte, rückwärtig eingebrachte Kristallreflexe säumen die aufbrechende Kerbung im spannungs-voll gerundeten Kristallkörper...

INSIDE SELECTING

One or more bold notches aligned symmetrically with the longitudinal axis signalize: the female sex. Playful crystal reflections added from the back line the notching as it breaks open in the tautly rounded crystal body...

NATURAL MOVEMENT

Das ästhetische Diktum der »Lupenreinheit« fällt: Die Materialität des Steins selbst wird zum Gegenstand der Betrachtung. Der Schliff setzt den Fokus auf die natürliche Kristallisation und die Einschlüsse im Mineral. Die plastische Gestaltung von Bernd Munsteiner arbeitet die farblichen Variationen und Verläufe heraus.

NATURAL MOVEMENT

The aesthetic dictates of ›purity‹ are set aside. The physical properties of the stone itself become the object of observation. The cut places the focus on natural crystallisation and the inclusions in the mineral. Bernd Munsteiner's sculptural working follows and enhances the variations in colour and their striation.

RHYTHMUS

Der gelegentlich sehr dynamische Verlauf der natürlichen Kristallisation fordert bei Bernd Munsteiner die materialgerechte Umsetzung heraus: Ein schmal glitzernder Katarakt aus rhythmisch getakteten Einschnitten zieht -- mal als *Crescendo*, mal als *Diminuendo* – seine Bahn in einem plan geschliffen erscheinenden Mineral.

RHYTHM

The occasionally very dynamic course taken by natural crystallisation challenges Bernd Munsteiner to translate it in a way that does full justice to the material: a narrow, glittering cataract of cuts measuring a rhythmic beat takes its course – sometimes rising to a *crescendo*, then again sinking to a *diminuendo* – in a mineral that looks as if it has been flat-cut.

METAMORPHOSE

Ein Bergkristall mit Rutilnadeln, die sich von einem imaginären Zentrum der Kristallisation wie ein Wirbelsturm ausbreiten. Transformation eines ursprünglich 850 kg schweren Naturwunders in eine »Metamorphose« betitelte Serie von freien, zum Teil spektakulär großen Skulpturen und Objekten.

METAMORPHOSIS

A rock crystal with needle-like rutile inclusions which spread out like a tornado from an imaginary centre of crystallisation. Transformation of what was originally a marvel of nature weighing 850 kg into a series of sculptures and objects, some of them of spectacular size, into a series entitled ›Meta-morphosis‹.

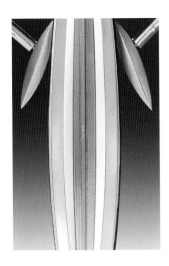

EROTIK

»Als ich am Anfang Kerben in Steine geschliffen habe, war das eine Revolution im Edelsteinschleifen. Die Kerbe war für mich ein Gestaltungsmittel. Und verbunden damit waren Assoziationen...« Seit Mitte der 1980er Jahre wird die Einkerbung in den Kristallen bei Bernd Munsteiner immer wieder zum Auslöser auch freizügiger erotischer Assoziationen.

EROTICISM

›When I first started cutting notches into stones, that was a revolution in gem-cutting. The notch was for me a means to forming and designing. And it was linked with associations ...‹ Since the mid-1980s notching in crystals has over and over again been the catalyst in Bernd Munsteiner's work for free associations which may also be erotic.

CONTEXT DIAMOND | SPIRIT DIAMOND

Unter Berücksichtigung der Totalreflexion aus der Grundform des natürlichen Diamantoktaeders entwickelte Schliffformen. »Spirit Diamond« zeigt den Schritt vom Quadrat zum Kreis mit einer im Ober- und im Unterteil von jeweils 16 Facetten. Die strahlenförmige Anordnung der gleich großen Facetten um den Mittelpunkt führt zu einer sehr hohen Bündelung des Lichts.

CONTEXT DIAMOND | SPIRIT DIAMOND

Forms of cutting that take into consideration the sum of reflections from the basic form of the natural diamond octahedron. ›Spirit Diamond‹ shows the step from square to circle with crown and pavilion composed of 16 facets each. The sunburst arrangement of the facets, which are of uniform size, induces a very strong concentration of light.

DOM PEDRO

Bislang größte künstlerische und technische Herausforderung für Bernd Munsteiner ist ein hellblauer, 26 kg schwerer Aquamarin. In sechs Monaten entsteht ein 35 cm hoher Obelisk – mit 10 363 ct der weltweit größte geschliffene Aquamarin. Wellenartige Einschnitte auf der Rückseite, »Ondas Maritimas«, spiegeln die Seele des Kristalls.

DOM PEDRO

To date the greatest artistic and technical challenge Bernd Munsteiner has faced is a light blue aquamarine weighing 26 kg. In six months a 35-cm-high obelisk emerged from it – at 10 363 ct the biggest cut aquamarine in the world. Wavy cuts on the back, ›Ondas Maritimas‹, reflect the soul of the crystal.

SYMBOLON

Die phallische Form lässt vordergründigen Raum für eine Deutung auf der erotischen Symbolebene. Die Ausformung als Lingam (indischer Kultstein) weist ihn allerdings als sakrales Objekt aus, das das weibliche und das männliche Prinzip vereint und so zugleich vom Werden und Vergehen, von Zeit und Ewigkeit kündet.

SYMBOLON

Viewed superficially, the phallic form leaves scope for interpretation on the plane of erotic symbolism. Since it has been formed into a Lingam (Indian cult stone), however, it is revealed as a sacral object uniting the female and the male principle and, therefore, heralding waxing and waning, time and infinity.

KRISTALLREFLEXIONEN

Die in quadratische Stahlplatten montierten Kompositionen aus geometrisch geschliffenen und angeordneten Bergkristallen oder Citrinen erinnern an die serielle Kunst oder Op-Art der 1960er Jahre. Für Bernd Munsteiner sind die »Tafelbilder« reflektierendes Fazit 40-jähriger Arbeit und zugleich Ausdruck künstlerischer Experimentierlust.

CRYSTAL REFLECTIONS

These compositions of geometrically cut and arranged rock crystals or citrines mounted in square steel plates recall 1960s Serial or Op art. To Bernd Munsteiner these ›Panel Pictures‹ represent the reflective summing up of forty years of work and at the same time express artistic delight in experimentation.

GLASOBJEKTE FÜR ROYAL COPENHAGEN

1991: Royal Copenhagen lädt den Kristallkünstler in die amorphe Welt des bunten Glases ein. Es bleibt ein eher kurzer Exkurs, doch künstlerisch keine Marginalie. Rund 50 zumeist kugel- oder stelenförmige, glutfarbene Klein-plastiken erzählen ihre vulkanische Genese im Prozess der Glasschmelze.

GLASS OBJECTS FOR ROYAL COPENHAGEN

1991: Royal Copenhagen invited the crystal artist into the amorphous world of coloured glass. This would turn out to be a rather brief digression yet, artistically speaking, it was anything but marginal. Roughly fifty mostly spherical or stele-shaped small sculptures in glowing colours tell of their volcanic genesis in the process of melting glass.

OBJEKTE IM AUSSENRAUM

Von der kristallinen Miniatur zur Skulptur in der Landschaft. Seit Ende der 1990er nimmt die Auseinandersetzung mit dem öffentlichen Raum zu. Es entstehen erste Stein-Zeichen mit kolorierten Einkerbungen in der heimatlichen Natur. »Blue Quartz Millennium 1999« ist eine tonnenschwere Skulptur aus blau gebändertem brasilianischen Quarz vor dem Neubau des Gemmological Institute of America in Kalifornien.

OUTDOOR OBJECTS

Ranging from the crystalline miniature to sculpture in landscape. The discussion with public space has increased since the late 1990s. Stone signs with coloured notches have been created in the natural environment of his native region. ›Blue Quartz Millennium 1999‹ is a sculpture of blue banded Brazilian quartz that weighs tonnes and stands in front of the new building of the Gemmological Institute of America in California.

WERKE

WORKS

DER GESCHLIFFENE KRISTALL WIRD ZUR
FREIEN PLASTIK, SUCHT SEINEN BEZUG ZUM
RAUM UND ZU SEINEM BETRACHTER.
SPIEGELNDE EINSCHNITTE AUS WECHSELNDEN
PERSPEKTIVEN – FÜR DAS UNGEÜBTE AUGE
ZUNÄCHST IRRITIERENDE REFLEKTIONEN DES
LICHTS – MACHEN DIE INNEREN UND ÄUSSEREN
PLASTISCHEN DIMENSIONEN DES KRISTALLS
ERFAHRBAR UND ERÖFFNEN NEUE UND
SPEKTAKULÄRE SEHRÄUME.

A CUT CRYSTAL HAS BECOME FREE SCULPTURE, SEEKING ITS RELATIONSHIP TO SPACE AND THOSE WHO LOOK AT IT. MIRRORING CUTS FROM CHANGING PERSPECTIVES – FOR THE UNPRACTISED EYE AT FIRST DISTURBING REFLECTIONS OF LIGHT – MAKE IT POSSIBLE TO EXPERIENCE THE INTERNAL AND EXTERNAL SCULPTURAL DIMENSIONS OF THE CRYSTAL, THUS OPENING NEW, SPECTACULAR VISUAL SPACES.

Bild | ZWEIDIMENSIONALE GESTALTUNG | 1966 | Sarderonyxreliefs || Picture | TWO-DIMENSIONAL DESIGN | 1966 | sardonyx reliefs

Bild | ZWEIDIMENSIONALE GESTALTUNG | 1966 | Sarderonyxreliefs || Picture | TWO-DIMENSIONAL DESIGN | 1966 | sardonyx reliefs

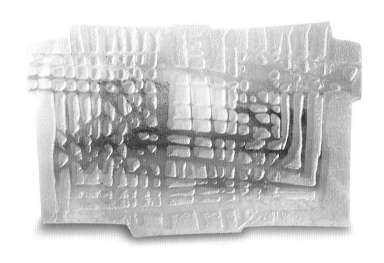

Brosche | Naturachatrelief | 1975 | Gold | Brillant || Brooch | natural agate relief | 1975 | gold | diamond

Halsschmuck | Carneolrelief | 1967 | Gold || Neck jewellery | cornelian relief | 1967 | gold

Brosche | Lagenachatrelief | 1969 | Gold | Granat | Brillant || Brooch | banded agate relief | 1969 | gold | garnet | diamond

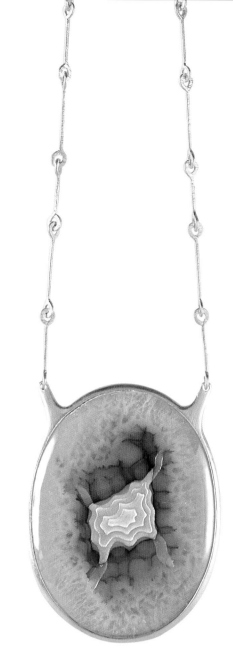

Halsschmuck | Naturachatrelief | 1977 | Gold || Neck jewellery | natural agate relief | 1977 | gold

Ring | Lagenachatrelief | 1975 | Gold || Ring | banded agate relief | 1975 | gold

Brosche | Naturachatrelief | 1977 | Gold | 3 Brillanten || Brooch | natural agate relief | 1977 | gold | 3 diamonds

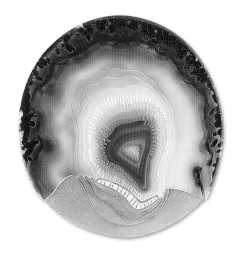

Bild | LANDSCHAFT | 1971 | Achatrelief || Picture | LANDSCAPE | 1971 | agate relief

Bild | LANDSCHAFT | 1978 | Achatrelief | Gold || Picture | LANDSCAPE | 1978 | agate relief | gold

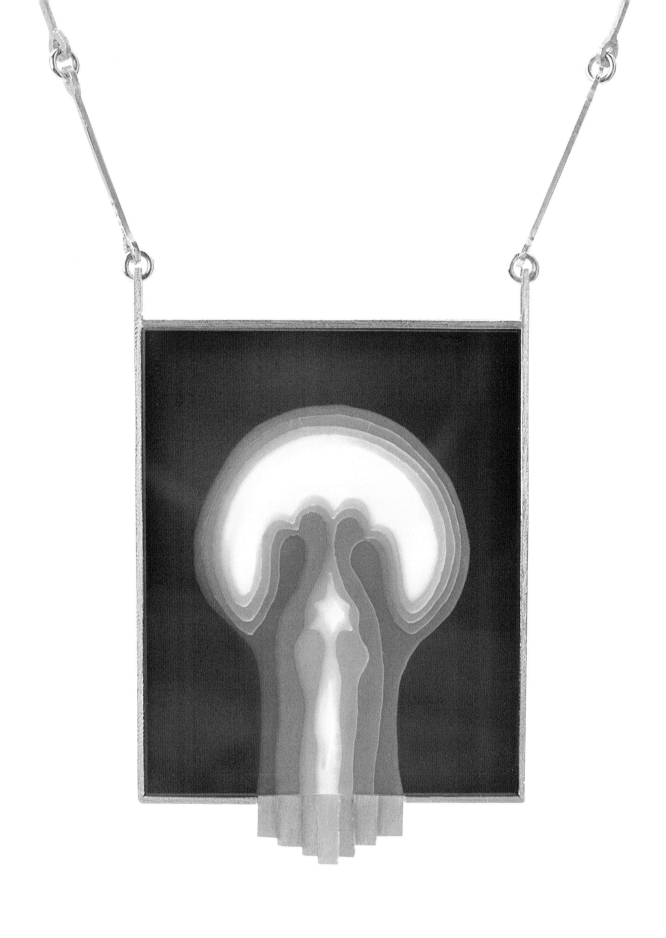

Halsschmuck | ANATOMISCHER QUERSCHNITT | 1976 | Sarderonyxrelief || Neck jewellery | ANATOMICAL SECTION | 1976 | sardonyx relief

Bild/Brosche | Sarderonyxrelief | 1978 | Gold | Smaragde || Picture/Brooch | sardonyx relief | 1978 | gold | emeralds

Bild | ANATOMISCHER QUERSCHNITT | 1976 | Sarderonyxrelief | Blattgold || Picture | ANATOMICAL SECTION | 1976 | sardonyx relief | gold leaf

1966–1979

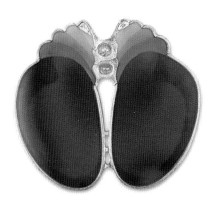

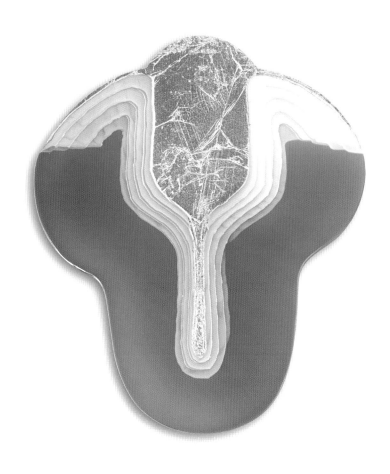

Bild | ANATOMISCHER QUERSCHNITT | 1979 | Sarderonyxrelief || Picture | ANATOMICAL SECTION | 1979 | sardonyx relief

Bild | ANATOMISCHER QUERSCHNITT | 1977 | Sarderonyxrelief | Blattgold || Picture | ANATOMICAL SECTION | 1977 | sardonyx relief | gold leaf

Bild | ANATOMISCHER QUERSCHNITT | 1977 | Sarderonyxrelief | Gold || Picture | ANATOMICAL SECTION | 1977 | sardonyx relief | gold

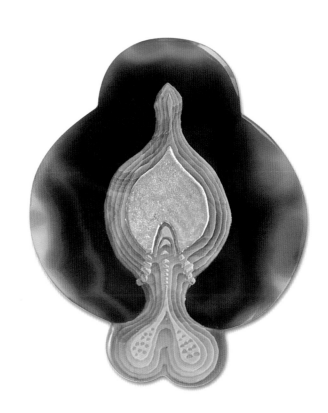

Ohrschmuck | D R E I E C K | 1979 | Onyxrelief | Gold | Platin | Diamant-Dreiecke || Ear jewellery | T R I A N G L E | 1979 | onyx relief | gold | platinum | diamond triangles

Halsschmuck | Achatrelief | 1979 | Gold | Brillant || Neck jewellery | agate relief | 1979 | gold | diamond

Manschettenknöpfe | Lagenachatreliefs | 1972 | Gold || Cuff-links | Banded Agate Reliefs | 1972 | gold

INSIDE SELECTING | 1979 | Rauchquarz 72,44 ct || INSIDE SELECTING | 1979 | smoky quartz 72.44 ct

Ring | INSIDE SELECTING | 1977 | Beryll | Gold || Ring | INSIDE SELECTING | 1977 | beryl | gold

REFLEKTIERENDE PERSPEKTIVEN MIT BOHRUNGEN | 1967 | Morganit 85,12 ct || REFLECTING PERSPECTIVES WITH BOREHOLES | 1967 | morganite 85.12 ct

REFLEKTIERENDE PERSPEKTIVEN | 1979 | Aquamarin 54,87 ct || REFLECTING PERSPECTIVES | 1979 | aquamarine 54.87 ct

REFLEKTIERENDE PERSPEKTIVEN | 1975 | Citrin 223,81 ct || REFLECTING PERSPECTIVES | 1975 | citrine 223.81 ct

INSIDE SELECTING | 1979 | Amethyst 37,28 ct || INSIDE SELECTING | 1979 | amethyst 37.28 ct

REFLEKTIERENDE PERSPEKTIVEN | 1969 | Turmalin 105,78 ct || REFLECTING PERSPECTIVES | 1969 | tourmaline 105.78 ct

REFLEKTIERENDE PERSPEKTIVEN | 1975 | Amethyst 84,08 ct || REFLECTING PERSPECTIVES | 1975 | amethyst 84.08 ct
REFLEKTIERENDE PERSPEKTIVEN | 1975 | Aquamarin 79,11 ct || REFLECTING PERSPECTIVES | 1975 | aquamarine 79.11 ct

REFLEKTIERENDE PERSPEKTIVEN | 1971 | Turmalin 37,57 ct || REFLECTING PERSPECTIVES | 1971 | tourmaline 37.57 ct
REFLEKTIERENDE PERSPEKTIVEN | 1971 | Citrin 104,76 ct || REFLECTING PERSPECTIVES | 1971 | citrine 104.76 ct

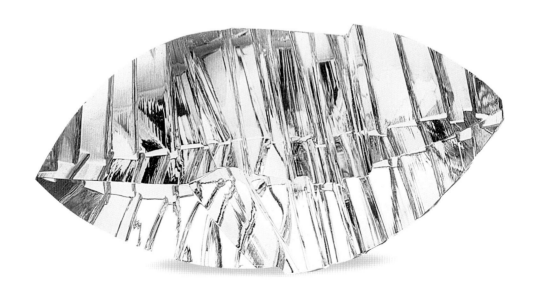

GETTING TO KNOW BERND
Si + Ann Frazier

The San Francisco Bay Area has long been known as a place whose denizens have not been afraid to ›think different.‹ However, actually getting paying customers to think different is not always so easy—even in Berkeley where I worked as an adolescent in a gem and mineral store. We sold stones cut in Idar-Oberstein but only in very conventional cuts which we bought from New York and Los Angeles dealers.

After graduating from University in the very early 1960s Ann and I determined to make a trip to Europe to visit mineral localities, collectors, and museums. We also visited Idar-Oberstein. There we had the good fortune to meet the late Georg Wild who let us camp out in his old agate cutting mill, so that we got time to really explore the area. We met many people prominent in the gem industry, fell in love with Idar, and vowed to return.

We, of course, did not meet, nor even hear of Bernd Munsteiner. He was still only a student in Pforzheim. His father and grandfather were cutters and Bernd first was

trained (1957–1960) to be an *Edelsteinschleifer* (gem cutter) too. He apprenticed to his father, Viktor Munsteiner, and received his journeyman's papers in 1960. He then studied at the Fachhochschule für Gestaltung in Pforzheim from 1962–1966. There he came under the influence of Prof. Schollmayer and Prof. Ullrich. He is quick to credit these professors for ›giving him wings and helping him learn to fly.‹ The thorough training in Art at the Fachhochschule enabled him to break free from the constraints of the traditional concepts of what lapidary art is. On the other hand the thorough grounding and mastery of the basic skills required of a professional gem cutter in Idar-Oberstein provided him with the tools to turn design concepts into hard rock reality.

While still a student he visited an exhibition held in the famous old glass working town of Gablonz (now Jablonec nad Nisou) in Bohemia in what is now the Czech Republic. Curiously enough that visit led indirectly to our becoming aware that there was a gem cutter and carver named Bernd Munsteiner. At Gablonz he discovered sandblasting, by means of which glass is configured. Using that quick insightful perception that has marked

UNSERE BEGEGNUNG MIT BERND
Si + Ann Frazier

Die Gegend um San Francisco ist seit langem dafür bekannt, dass ihre Bewohner sich nie gescheut haben, Anders-Denkende zu sein. Dennoch ist es nicht immer so einfach, aus zahlenden Kunden Querdenker zu machen – sogar in Berkeley, wo ich als Jugendlicher in einem Edelstein- und Mineralienladen arbeitete. Wir verkauften in Idar-Oberstein geschliffene Steine, aber nur in sehr konventionellen Schliffen, die wir von Händlern aus New York oder Los Angeles kauften.

Nach meinem Universitätsabschluss in den frühen 1960er Jahren beschlossen Ann und ich, nach Europa zu reisen, um dort Orte, an denen es Mineralien gab, sowie Sammler und Museen, die sich mit Mineralien beschäftigten, zu besuchen. Wir fuhren auch nach Idar-Oberstein. Dort hatten wir das Glück, den inzwischen verstorbenen Georg Wild zu treffen, der uns in seiner alten Achat-Schleiferei zelten ließ, so dass wir Zeit hatten, die Gegend richtig zu erkunden. Wir trafen viele in der Edelstein-Branche wichtige und einflussreiche Menschen, verliebten uns in Idar und versprachen, wiederzukommen.

Natürlich trafen wir Bernd Munsteiner damals nicht, noch hörten wir von ihm. Er war zu der Zeit noch Student in Pforzheim. Sein Vater und Großvater waren Edelstein-schleifer, und auch Bernd machte von 1957 bis 1960 zunächst eine Ausbildung zum Edelsteinschleifer. Er ging bei seinem Vater, Viktor Munsteiner, in die Lehre und machte 1960 seinen Gesellenbrief. Von 1962 bis 1966 studierte er an der Fachhochschule für Gestaltung in Pforzheim, wo er vor allem von Prof. Schollmayer und Prof. Ullrich beeinflusst wurde. Er betont gerne und oft, dass diese Professoren ihm »Flügel verliehen und zeigten, wie man fliegen lernt«. Durch die gründliche Schulung im Fach Kunst an der Fachhochschule war es ihm möglich, sich von den eingeschränkten traditionellen Vorstellungen, was Edelsteinschleifkunst ist, frei zu machen. Andererseits ermöglichte ihm die Tatsache, dass er die grundlegenden Fertigkeiten, die von einem fachmännischen Edelsteinschleifer verlangt werden, beherrschte: Gestaltungs-Vorstellungen in steinerne Wirklichkeit zu verwandeln.

Noch als Student besuchte Munsteiner eine Ausstellung, die in der berühmten alten Glashüttenstadt Gablonz in Böhmen (jetzt Jablonec nad Nisou in der Tschechischen Republik) stattfand. Erstaunlicherweise führte dieser Besuch indirekt dazu, dass wir von dem Edelsteinschleifer und Steinschneider Bernd Munsteiner erfuhren. In Gablonz entdeckte er das Sandstrahlgebläse, mit dem Glas gestaltet wurde. Aufgrund seiner schnellen Auffassungsgabe, die Bernds künstlerische Karriere grundsätzlich bestimmte, erkannte er die Möglichkeit, mit Hilfe dieser Technik, Achat auf eine radikal andere Art und Weise zu bearbeiten. Nachdem er 1966 die Fachhochschule mit dem Staatsexamen als Gestalter für Edelsteine und Schmuck abgeschlossen hatte, kehrte er mit seiner Verlobten nach Stipshausen zurück und richtete dort seine eigene Werkstatt ein. Zu Beginn wurden seine unkonventionellen Edelsteine in Idar-Oberstein mit beträchtlicher Skepsis betrachtet, aber 1967 begann er, Steine nach Dänemark und England zu verkaufen. Von Bernds kunstvoll geschliffenen Achaten, Onyxen und Karneolen war – etwa um die gleiche Zeit – jemand so beeindruckt, dass das Heimatmuseum (jetzt Museum Idar-Oberstein unterhalb der Felsenkirche) einige von ihnen ausstellte. In den frühen 1970er Jahren hatten wir den Stein- und Mineralienladen in Berkeley, in dem ich als Student gearbeitet hatte, gekauft, und wir begannen, zwei Mal im Jahr nach Idar zu fahren, um dort geschliffene Steine für unser schnell wachsendes Geschäft für Juwelier- und Goldschmiedebedarf zu kaufen. Bei einem Besuch im Heimatmuseum sahen wir diese wundervollen Kunstwerke aus Achat, und da wir leidenschaftliche Sammler von Achaten sind, waren wir vollkommen begeistert. Wir machten Fotos von ihnen und illustrierten damit unsere vielen Vorträge. Irgendwie kamen wir aber nie auf die Idee, Bernd Munsteiner persönlich ausfindig zu machen und ein paar von den Achaten zu kaufen. Wir dachten, wir hätten nicht das nötige Geld für einen solchen Kauf, und obwohl wir sie liebten, glaubten wir, dass sie sich nicht verkaufen würden. Nun, zumindest wissen wir, dass wir mit der ersten Annahme ziemlich richtig lagen.

Bernd's artistic career, he saw an opportunity to do something radically different with agate. After he had graduated and passed the state exam for gemstone and jewelry design and creation [Staatsexamen als Gestalter für Edelsteine und Schmuck] in 1966, he returned with his bride to Stipshausen and set up his own studio. At first his unconventional gemstones created considerable skepticism in Idar-Oberstein, but in 1967 he started selling stones to Denmark and England. Somewhere about this time someone was impressed enough with Bernd's artistically abraded agate, onyx, and carnelian agates that the Heimat Museum (now the Museum Idar-Oberstein unterhalb der Felsenkirche) put some on display. By the early 1970s we had bought the gem and mineral shop in Berkeley, where I had worked as a student and we started traveling to Idar twice a year to buy cut stones for our rapidly growing jeweler's supply business. On a visit to the Heimat Museum we saw those wonderful agate works of art, and because we are ardent agate collectors we were totally blown away. We took pictures of them which we used to illustrate our frequent lectures. Somehow the idea never occurred to us to try to track Bernd Munsteiner down and purchase some. We figured that we did not have enough money to make a purchase, and though we loved them, felt that they would not sell. Well, at least we know we were pretty safe with the first assumption. The second erroneous assumption is one more reason why we are not wealthy.

Meanwhile Bernd started winning prizes and write-ups about his innovative gem cutting began to appear in magazines. We began to hear questions about him and we slowly came to the realization that he was a very important sensation in the gemstone and jewelry world. Looking back with 20-20 hindsight we realize that we really missed the boat. By the mid-1970s Munsteiner's radical new vision of gemstone cutting was beginning to have an effect on the whole industry and nowhere more so than the San Francisco Bay Area. In 1981 there was even a show of Munsteiner's work at the Contemporary Artisans Gallery in San Francisco. Anne Grundler, who had been the Munsteiner's hostess during their stay, was an old acquaintance of ours who we would meet at local gem and mineral shows. She kept us up with Bernd's skyrocketing popularity with the crème de la crème of San

Francisco Bay Area jewelers. It was about this time that we closed our large volume (for the time) gem wholesale business to devote ourselves to writing, teaching, and travelling. Meanwhile Bernd Munsteiner was becoming a hero and icon for every serious San Francisco jewelry craftsperson/artist. On our regular trips to Idar we came to recognize him from his appearances at the Intergem show and at the German Gemological Association meetings. We met him and found him to be very affable and charming. In the 1990s Bernd had received considerable coverage in the international trade press for several free-standing unique gem sculptures that were of a size not to be considered, even by a Valkyrie, as jewelry. As mineral collectors with a special interest in quartz, we were absolutely fascinated by these sculptures. We have always strongly believed that large, fine quality pieces of gem rough are great rarities of Nature and should be preserved for future generations to enjoy. Unfortunately, as we so well know from our own years in the gem business, cutting a big piece of gem rough into many small, readily salable gemstones makes much more sense than to try and preserve the unique large piece as an individual specimen. We

were thrilled to see that there was now a renowned gem cutter who had the courage to resist this previously implacable ›law‹ of gemstone economics.

In the Spring of 1990 Munsteiner completed work on a giant gem sculpture called ›Metamorphosis‹. It is a stunning work of gem art. The complete piece weighs 97.2 kilograms (214.3 pounds) and was cut from a crystal weighing 830 kilograms (1,830 pounds). The original crystal was the finest large rutilated quartz crystal Munsteiner (or anyone else we know) had even seen. We were delighted when our editor, Merle White, at the *Lapidary Journal*, agreed that ›Metamorphosis‹ would make a great article. It appeared with a fine cover picture in the February, 1991 issue. We had the great privilege of conducting a long, taped interview with Bernd at his stunningly beautiful studio in Stipshausen in the hills above Idar-Oberstein. Because of Bernd's wit, charm, and encyclopedic knowledge of all aspects of gems, gem cutting, the gem trade, and art, it was one of the most enjoyable interviews we have ever conducted.

There is a happy ending to this story. The sculpture was acquired by a California collector who believes in letting

Die zweite, irrtümliche Annahme ist einer der Gründe, warum wir nicht reich sind.

In der Zwischenzeit gewann Bernd erste Preise, und es erschienen zunehmend Presseberichte über seinen innovativen Edelsteinschliff in Zeitschriften. Leute fragten uns nach ihm, und uns wurde langsam klar, dass er eine Sensation in der Welt der Steine und des Schmucks war. Wenn wir nun mit klarem Blick zurückschauen, erkennen wir, dass wir wirklich den Anschluss verpasst haben. Mitte der 1970er Jahre begann Munsteiners radikal neue Sicht des Steinschliffs die gesamte Branche zu beeinflussen – und das ganz besonders in der Gegend um San Francisco. 1981 wurden Munsteiners Arbeiten sogar in der Contemporary Artisans Gallery [Galerie für zeitgenössische angewandte Kunst] in San Francisco gezeigt. Anne Grundler, Gastgeberin der Munsteiners während ihres Aufenthalts, war eine alte Bekannte von uns, die wir oft auf den örtlichen Edelstein- und Mineralienmessen trafen. Sie hielt uns über Bernds rasant zunehmende Beliebtheit bei der *Crème de la Crème* der Juweliere in San Francisco und Umgebung auf dem Laufenden. Etwa um diese Zeit schlossen wir unseren (für diese Zeit) sehr umsatzstarken Stein-Großhandel, um uns dem Schreiben, Unterrichten und Reisen zu widmen. In der Zwischenzeit wurde Bernd Munsteiner Held und Ikone für alle, die sich in San Francisco auf handwerklicher oder künstlerischer Ebene ernsthaft mit Schmuck beschäftigten. Auf unseren regelmäßigen Reisen nach Idar begannen wir ihn durch seine Auftritte auf der Intergem-Messe und den Treffen des Bundesverbands der Edelstein- und Diamantindustrie kennen zu lernen. Wir trafen uns mit ihm und fanden ihn sehr umgänglich und charmant.

In den 1990er Jahren war in der internationalen Presse eine Reihe von Berichten über einige von Bernds frei stehenden einzigartigen Edelsteinskulpturen erschienen, die man aufgrund ihrer Größe beim besten Willen nicht mehr als Schmuck bezeichnen konnte. Als Mineralien-Sammler mit besonderem Interesse an Quarz waren wir absolut fasziniert von diesen Skulpturen. Wir waren immer der festen Überzeugung, dass große, schöne Rohsteine wunderbare Seltenheiten der Natur sind und für zukünftige Generationen erhalten werden sollten, damit auch diese sich noch daran erfreuen können. Wie wir aus unseren eigenen jahrelangen Erfahrungen im Edelstein-Geschäft nur zu gut wissen, macht es ökonomisch aber leider viel mehr Sinn, aus einem großen Stück Rohstein viele kleine, leicht verkäufliche Steine zu schneiden, als zu versuchen, das große Mineral als eigenständiges Stück zu erhalten. Wir waren hoch erfreut zu sehen, dass es nun einen renommierten Edelsteinschleifer gab, der den Mut hatte, sich diesem bisher unangreifbaren »Gesetz« des Edelsteinmarktes zu widersetzen.

Im Frühjahr 1990 beendete Munsteiner eine riesige Steinskulptur mit dem Titel »Metamorphose«. Es ist ein atemberaubendes Werk der Edelstein-Kunst. Das gesamte Stück wiegt 97,2 kg und wurde aus einem 830 kg schweren Kristall geschliffen. Der ursprüngliche Stein war der schönste und größte Bergkristall mit Rutil, den Munsteiner (und alle anderen Leute, die wir kennen) jemals gesehen hatte. Wir waren glücklich, dass Merle White, unsere Herausgeberin beim *Lapidary Journal*, wie wir der Meinung war, dass man einen großartigen Artikel über die Arbeit »Metamorphose« schreiben konnte. Dieser erschien in der Februar-Ausgabe 1991 mit einem schönen Cover-Foto. Es war uns eine große Ehre, ein langes, auf Tonband aufgenommenes Interview mit Bernd in seinem wunderschönen Atelier in Stipshausen in den Hügeln über Idar-Oberstein zu führen. Bernds Witz, sein Charme und sein enzyklopädisches Wissen über alles, was mit Edelsteinen, Steinschliff, Mineralien-Handel und Kunst zu tun hat, machten es zu einem der Interviews, die wir am meisten genossen.

Die Geschichte der »Metamorphose« hat ein Happy End. Die Skulptur wurde von einem kalifornischen Sammler gekauft, der die Öffentlichkeit an seinen Schätzen teilhaben lässt. Wir hatten das große persönliche Vergnügen, dieses wunderbare Stück in einer Sonderausstellung in einem Museum in Los Angeles zu sehen. Wir sind glücklich, dass es sich dauerhaft in Kalifornien befindet und dass es durch einen speziellen, raffiniert gestalteten Sockelkasten vor der berüchtigten geologischen Instabilität der kalifornischen Erdkruste geschützt wird.

Dennoch haben wir das vielleicht schönste Kunstwerk aus Edelstein, von dem wir je hörten, aus den Augen verloren. Wir denken, dass es sich vielleicht noch in Idar befindet,

the public see his treasures. We had the great personal pleasure recently of seeing this wonder on display in a special exhibition in a Los Angeles museum. We are happy that it is permanently in California and that it resides in a special case cleverly designed to protect it from that notorious geological instability of the California crust.

Perhaps the finest work of art in gemstones that we have ever heard of, however, has dropped from our sight. We think it might still be in Idar but are not sure. It is an extraordinary sculpture created from an amazingly large gem aquamarine crystal of enormous pecuniary value. Again we were lucky enough to be able to interview Bernd about this magnum opus. The magnificent single, hexagonal crystal from which it was cut was 59 cm tall (nearly 2 feet!) and 16.5 cm (6.5 inches) in diameter. Before cutting it weighted an astounding 25.88 kilograms (nearly 60 pounds). The crystal was a gemmy, greenish-blue aquamarine color and was almost clean except for an area of tubes near the top which, however, Bernd used to great artistic advantage.

Bernd's first comment regarding the final sculpture was that ›the opportunity to work on such a crystal will nev-er happen again.‹ No single gem firm could afford to buy this magnificent piece of gem rough, so a consortium of dealers, after many difficulties, (detailed in our article in the *Lapidary Journal*, November, 1995) was able to bring it to Idar-Oberstein. From it, Bernd and his helpers in his studio produced a carving called ›Dom Pedro – Ondas Maritimas,‹ honoring Brazil's first two monarchs, Dom Pedro I and Dom Pedro II. The finished sculpture weighs nearly five pounds—roughly ten times more than its nearest competitor—stands almost 14 inches tall and measures over four inches wide at the base. ›Dom Pedro‹ holds the record as the world's largest cut and polished gem aquamarine to date.

It is hard to believe that either ›Metamorphose‹ or ›Dom Pedro‹ will ever be matched but if they ever are, Bernd Munsteiner will deserve much of the credit for showing the way.

Unlike so many famous artists Bernd does not try to protect himself from competitors. In fact, he is likely to work hard to show them the way and share his know-ledge. He believes in and is excited about his art and he wants others to share his excitement and insights.

In the Spring of 2000 Bernd flew to San Francisco to present his insights to a class drawn from all over the U.S. and Canada at the famous Revere Academy of Jewelry Arts. We were extremely envious of the students who were able to take this class. He chose as a theme: how to take advantage of inclusions in a piece of rough. He brought with him pieces of included rough quartz for each of the students to work on. By the end of the class each student had produced a fine gemstone carving. Alan Revere allowed us to sneak into class a couple of times. We remember Bernd, a natural teacher, at the front of the class holding up a piece of quartz with prominent inclusions and asking, ›Is it a flaw or an opportunity?‹ A simple question, but the answer to this question was profoundly different for all of the students five days later.

sind aber nicht sicher. Es ist eine außergewöhnliche Skulptur aus einem unglaublich großen Aquamarin-Kristall von enormem Wert. Wir hatten wiederum das Glück, Bernd zu diesem *opus magnum* interviewen zu können. Der prachtvolle hexagonale Kristall, aus dem die Plastik geschliffen wurde, war 59 cm hoch und hatte einen Durchmesser von 16,5 cm. Vor dem Schliff wog er erstaunliche 25,88 kg. Der Kristall war von funkelnder, grünlich-blauer aquamariner Farbe und fast vollständig klar – außer am oberen Ende, wo sich kleine Hohlräume befanden. In seiner großartigen künstlerischen Bearbeitung aber machte sich Bernd genau das zunutze. Bernds erster Kommentar über diese letzte Skulptur war, dass »es nie wieder die Möglichkeit geben wird, an einem solchen Kristall zu arbeiten«. Eine einzelne Edelsteinfirma konnte sich den Kauf dieses wunderbaren unbearbeiteten Steins nicht leisten, deshalb gelang es – nach vielen Schwierigkeiten – erst einem Konsortium von Händlern (die wir in unserem Artikel im *Lapidary Journal*, November 1995, ausführlich schilderten), ihn nach Idar-Oberstein zu bringen. Daraus schufen Bernd und seine Helfer in der Werkstatt eine Skulptur namens »Dom Pedro – Ondas Maritimas« – zu Ehren von Brasiliens ersten beiden Monarchen, Dom Pedro I und Dom Pedro II. Die fertige Skulptur wiegt fast 5 Pfund – etwa zehn Mal mehr als die, die ihr am nächsten kommt –, ist fast 35 cm hoch und am Sockel mehr als 10 cm breit. »Dom Pedro« hält bis heute den Rekord als weltweit größter geschliffener Aquamarin in Edelsteinqualität.

Es ist schwer vorstellbar, dass es je etwas mit »Metamorphose« oder »Dom Pedro« Vergleichbares geben wird, aber wenn doch, wird es Bernd Munsteiners Verdienst sein, ein Vorreiter gewesen zu sein.

Im Gegensatz zu so vielen berühmten Künstlern versucht Bernd nicht, sich vor Konkurrenten zu schützen. Er würde wohl sogar eher hart arbeiten, um ihnen den Weg zu weisen und sein Wissen zu teilen. Er glaubt an seine Kunst und ist von ihr so begeistert, dass er andere Menschen an dieser Begeisterung und seinen Einblicken teilhaben lassen möchte.

Im Frühjahr 2000 flog Bernd nach San Francisco, um an der berühmten Revere Academy of Jewelry Arts sein Wissen einer Gruppe von Studenten aus den ganzen USA und Kanada weiterzugeben. Wir beneideten diese Studenten sehr darum, sein Seminar belegen zu können. Sein Thema lautete: »Wie man sich Einschlüsse in einem Rohling zunutze macht«. Er brachte Stücke rohen Quarzes mit Einlagerungen mit, an denen jeder Student arbeiten konnte. Am Ende des Seminars hatten alle einen schönen Edelsteinschliff geschaffen. Alan Revere erlaubte uns, ein paar Mal unerkannt am Unterricht teilzunehmen. Wir erinnern uns an Bernd, einen geborenen Lehrer, wie er vor der Klasse ein Stück Quarz mit gut erkennbaren Einschlüssen in die Höhe hält und fragt: »Ist das ein Mangel oder eine Chance?« Eine einfache Frage, aber die Antwort darauf war für die Studenten fünf Tage später eine völlig andere.

Bild | Naturachatrelief | 1980 || Picture | natural agate relief | 1980

Bild | LANDSCHAFT | 1980 | Achatrelief || Picture | LANDSCAPE | 1980 | agate relief

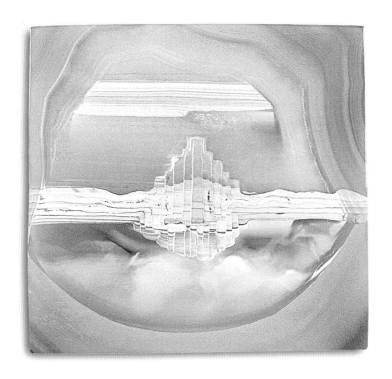

Bild | FIEBERKURVE I | 1986 | Sarderonyxrelief | Silber || Picture | FEVER CURVE I | 1986 | sardonyx relief | silver

Bild | FAMILIEN | 1984 | Sarderonyxrelief || Picture | FAMILIES | 1984 | sardonyx relief

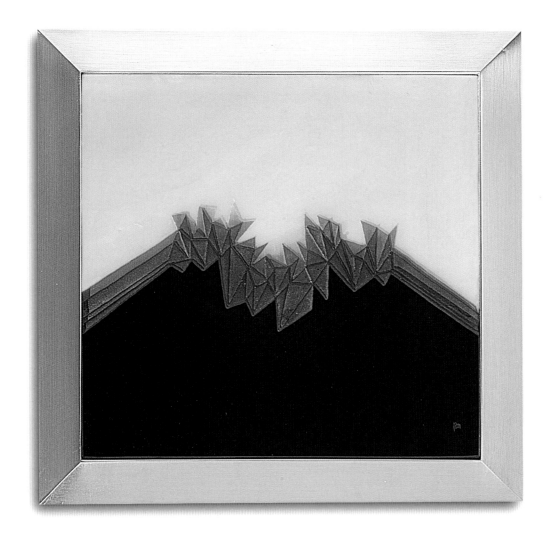

Halsschmuck | DREIECK | 1982 | Sarderonyxrelief | Gold | Silber | Schmuckgestaltung: Jörg Munsteiner || Neck jewellery | TRIANGLE | 1982 | sardonyx relief | gold | silver | Jewellery design: Jörg Munsteiner

Bild | LANDSCHAFT | 1986 | Sarderonyxrelief | Silber || Picture | LANDSCAPE | 1986 | sardonyx relief | silver

Bild/Brosche | EROTIK | 1989 | Sarderonyxrelief | Gold | Platin | Brillant || Picture/Brooch | EROTICISM | 1989 | sardonyx relief | gold | platinum | diamond

Ring | Lagenachatrelief | 1986 | Gold | Brillant || Ring | banded agate relief | 1986 | gold | diamond

Skulptur | MEDITATION | 1987 | Citrin | Gold | Rauchquarz | Silber | Michael M. Scott Collection || Sculpture | MEDITATION | 1987 | citrine | gold | smoky quartz | silver | Michael M. Scott Collection

Halsschmuck | REFLEKTIERENDE PERSPEKTIVEN | 1987 | Amethyst | Onyxrelief | Brillanten | Gold | Leder || Neck jewellery | REFLECTING PERSPECTIVES | 1987 | amethyst | onyx relief | diamonds | gold | leather

Brosche | Turmalin | Achatrelief | 1986 | Gold || Brooch | agate relief | 1986 | tourmaline | gold

REFLEKTIERENDE PERSPEKTIVEN | 1984 | Aquamarin 19,55 ct || REFLECTING PERSPECTIVES | 1984 | aquamarine 19.55 ct

REFLEKTIERENDE PERSPEKTIVEN | 1988 | Aquamarin 54,40 ct || REFLECTING PERSPECTIVES | 1988 | aquamarine 54.40 ct

REFLEKTIERENDE PERSPEKTIVEN | 1986 | Citrin 154,54 ct || REFLECTING PERSPECTIVES | 1986 | citrine 154.54 ct

REFLEKTIERENDE PERSPEKTIVEN | 1981 | Edeltopas 7,40 ct || REFLECTING PERSPECTIVES | 1981 | precious topaz 7.40 ct

REFLEKTIERENDE PERSPEKTIVEN | 1980 | Citrin 52,16 ct || REFLECTING PERSPECTIVES | 1980 | citrine 52.16 ct

INSIDE SELECTING | 1986 | Amethyst/Citrin 46,20 ct || INSIDE SELECTING | 1986 | amethyst/citrine 46.20 ct

INSIDE SELECTING | 1984 | Citrin 293,16 ct || INSIDE SELECTING | 1984 | citrine 293.16 ct

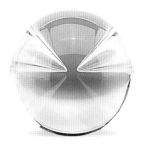

INSIDE SELECTING | 1987 | Beryll 49,61 ct || INSIDE SELECTING | 1987 | beryl 49.61 ct

Skulptur | KEGEL | 1987 | Bergkristall | Citrin || Sculpture | CONES | 1987 | rock crystal | citrine

INSIDE SELECTING | 1988 | Amethyst/Citrin 37,38 ct || INSIDE SELECTING | 1988 | amethyst/citrine 37.38 ct

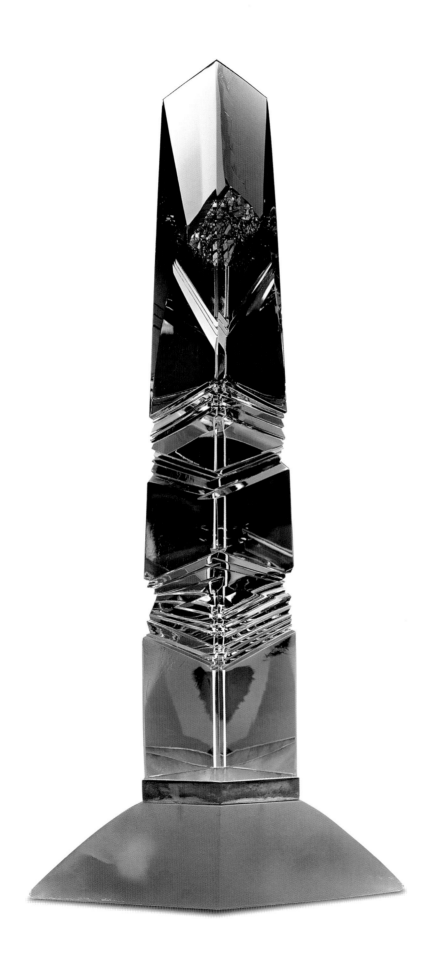

Skulptur | NATURAL MOVEMENT | 1985 | Rauchquarz | Silber | H 35 cm || Sculpture | NATURAL MOVEMENT | 1985 | smoky quartz | silver | H 35 cm

Skulptur | REFLEKTIERENDE PERSPEKTIVEN V | 1988 | Rauchquarz | Bergkristall | Silber | Michael M. Scott Collection || Sculpture |
REFLECTING PERSPECTIVES V | 1988 | smoky quartz | rock crystal | silver | Michael M. Scott Collection

Skulptur | IMPRESSIONEN | 1988 | Rauchquarz | Bergkristall | Silber | Michael M. Scott Collection | Sculpture | IMPRESSIONS | 1988 | smoky quartz | rock crystal | silver | Michael M. Scott Collection

Skulptur | NATURAL MOVEMENT III | 1987 | Rauchquarz mit Rutil | Obsidian | Silber | Michael M. Scott Collection | Sculpture | NATURAL MOVEMENT III | 1987 | smoky quartz with rutile | obsidian | silver | Michael M. Scott Collection

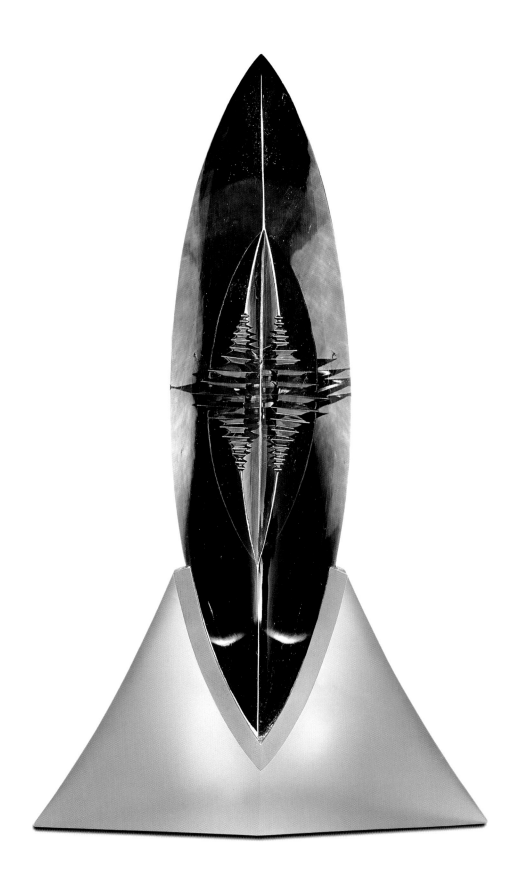

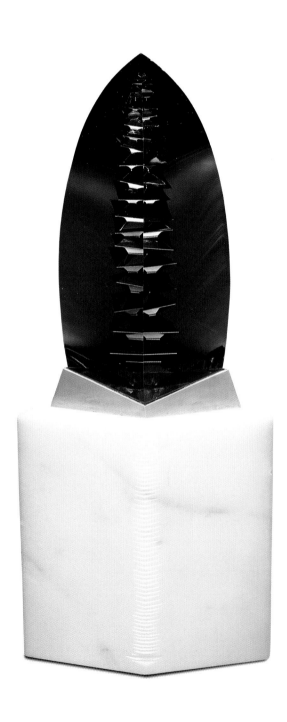

Skulptur | R H Y T H M U S II | 1989 | Amethyst | Marmor | Gold | Michael M. Scott Collection || Sculpture | R H Y T H M II | 1989 | amethyst | marble | gold | Michael M. Scott Collection

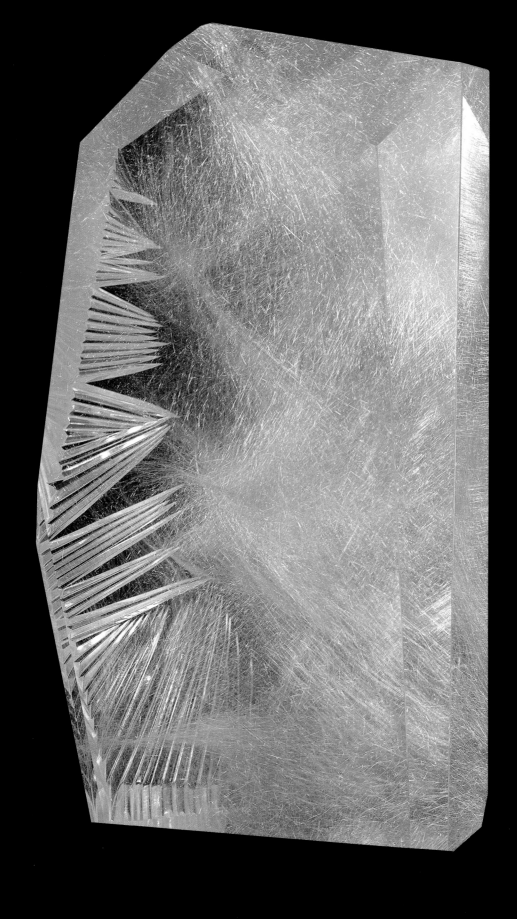

AM ANFANG STEHT DER JAHRHUNDERTFUND
EINES 850 KG SCHWEREN KRISTALLS: DER
BERGKRISTALL BIRGT EINEN WIRBEL VON
RUTILNADELN, DIE SICH VON EINEM
IMAGINÄREN ZENTRUM AUS DURCH DEN
GANZEN STEIN HINDURCH AUSBREITEN.
EINE EINZIGARTIGE SERIE VON GROSSEN
SKULPTUREN UND KLEINEREN OBJEKTEN
INSZENIERT DAS DRAMATISCHE NATUR-
SCHAUSPIEL DER »METAMORPHOSE«.

AT THE BEGINNING THERE WAS A CRYSTAL
WEIGHING 850 KG, A FIND THAT MAY OCCUR
ONCE IN A HUNDRED YEARS: THE ROCK
CRYSTAL CONCEALS A SWIRL OF NEEDLE-LIKE
RUTILE INCLUSIONS WHICH SPREAD
THROUGHOUT THE STONE FROM AN IMAGINARY
CENTRE. AN UNPRECEDENTED SERIES OF LARGE
SCULPTURES AND SMALLER OBJECTS STAGES
THE DRAMATIC NATURAL SPECTACLE OF
>METAMORPHOSIS<.

Skulptur | METAMORPHOSE I | 1990 | Bergkristall mit Rutil | Michael M. Scott Collection || Sculpture | METAMORPHOSIS I | 1990 | rock crystal
with rutile | Michael M. Scott Collection

1990–1993

Skulptur | METAMORPHOSE II | 1990 | Bergkristall mit Rutil | H 54 cm || Sculpture | METAMORPHOSIS II | 1990 | rock crystal with rutile | H 54 cm

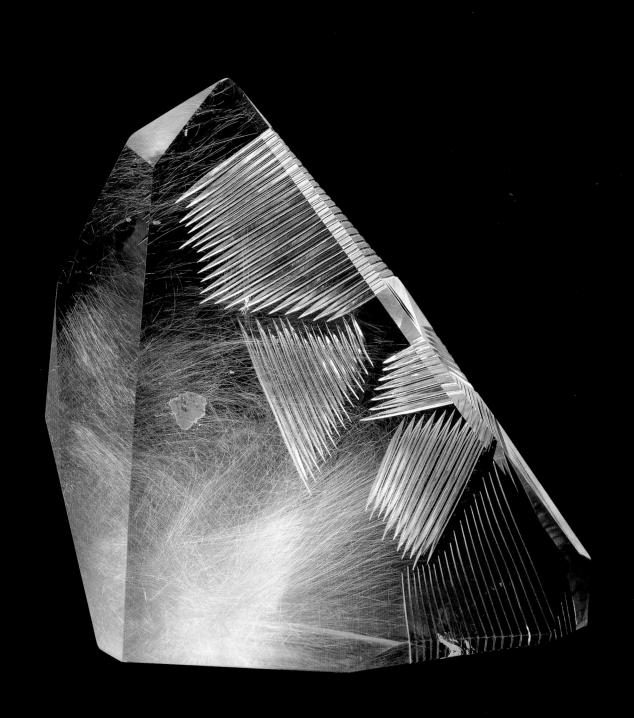

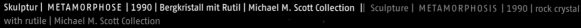

Skulptur | METAMORPHOSE | 1990 | Bergkristall mit Rutil | Michael M. Scott Collection || Sculpture | METAMORPHOSIS | 1990 | rock crystal with rutile | Michael M. Scott Collection

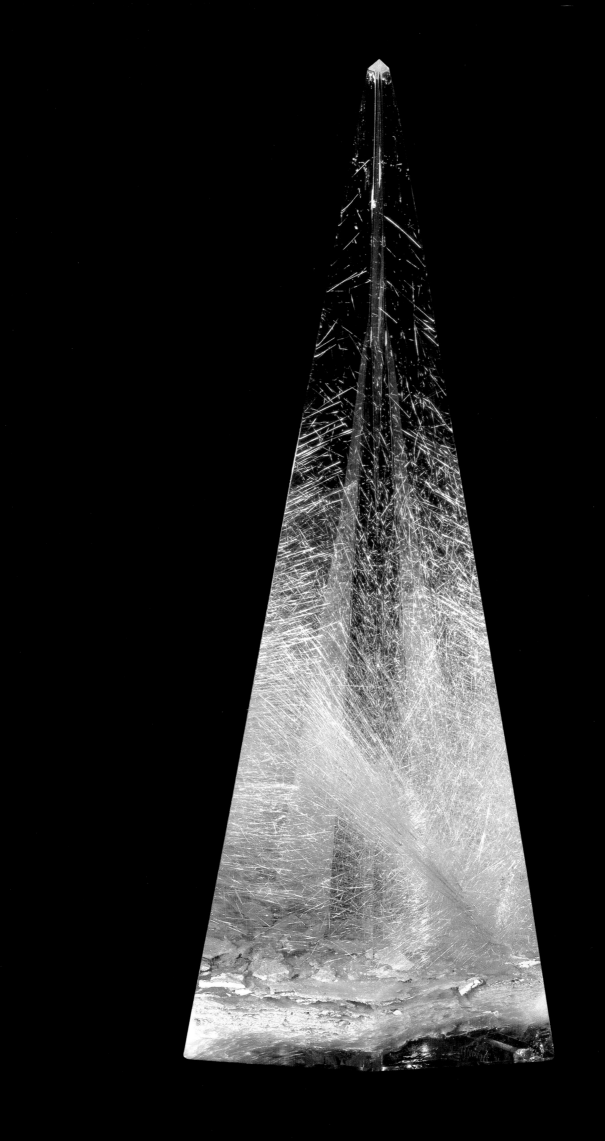

REFLEKTIERENDE PERSPEKTIVEN | 1992 | Aquamarin 59,39 ct || REFLECTING PERSPECTIVES | 1992 | aquamarine 59.39 ct

INSIDE SELECTING | 1992 | Aquamarin 109,05 ct || INSIDE SELECTING | 1992 | aquamarine 109.05 ct

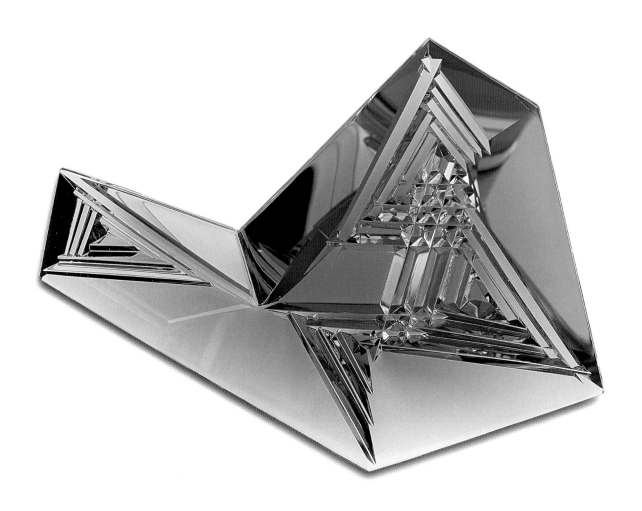

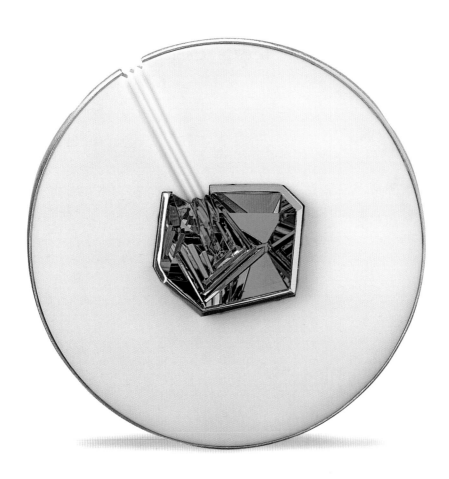

Objekt/Brosche | REFLEKTIERENDE PERSPEKTIVEN | 1990 | Turmalin | Achatrelief | Gold | Citrin || Object/Brooch | REFLECTING PERSPECTIVES | 1990 | tourmaline | agate relief | gold | citrine

REFLEKTIERENDE PERSPEKTIVEN | 1991 | Aquamarin 34,46 ct || REFLECTING PERSPECTIVES | 1991 | aquamarine 34.46 ct

Brosche | REFLEKTIERENDE PERSPEKTIVEN | 1991 | Amethyst | Achatrelief | Gold || Brooch | REFLECTING PERSPECTIVES | 1991 | amethyst | agate relief | gold

REFLEKTIERENDE PERSPEKTIVEN | 1992 | Turmalin 113,89 ct | Michael M. Scott Collection || REFLECTING PERSPECTIVES | 1992 | tourmaline 113.89 ct | Michael M. Scott Collection

Skulptur | COMPOSITION NEGATIVSCHNITTE | 1991 | Bergkristall mit Rutil | Aluminium | Michael M. Scott Collection || Sculpture | COMPOSITION NEGATIVE CUTS | 1991 | rock crystal with rutile | aluminium | Michael M. Scott Collection

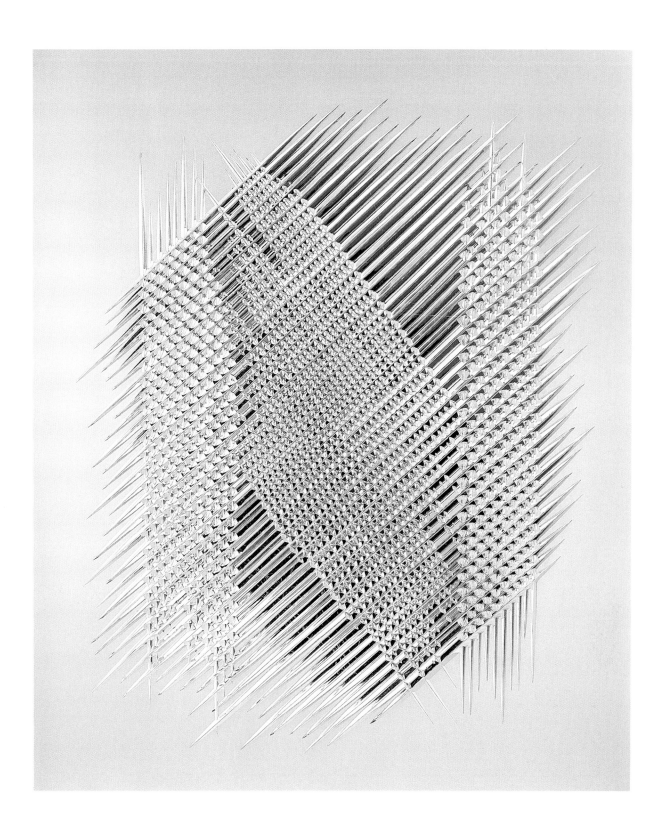

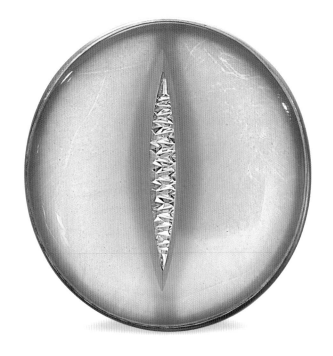

Brosche | EROTIK | 1993 | Aquamarin | Platin || Brooch | EROTICISM | 1993 | aquamarine | platinum

Brosche | EROTIK | 1992 | Citrin | Gold || Brooch | EROTICISM | 1992 | citrine | Silber | gold

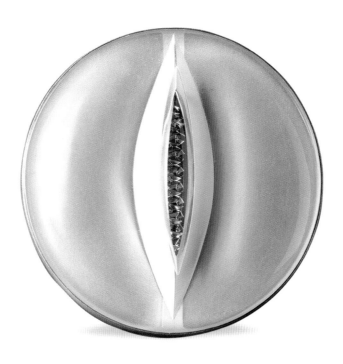

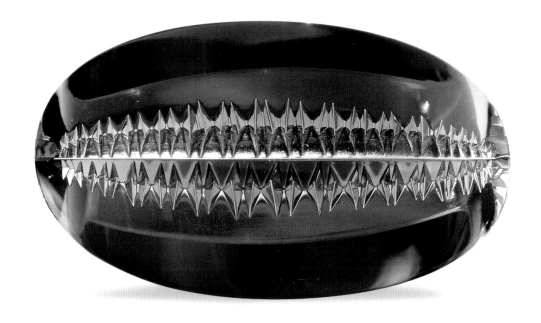

INSIDE SELECTING | 1992 | Amethyst 360,70 ct | Michael M. Scott Collection || INSIDE SELECTING | 1992 | amethyst 360.70 ct | Michael M. Scott Collection

Halsschmuck | INSIDE SELECTING | 1991 | Citrin | Brillanten | Gold | Platin || Neck jewellery | INSIDE SELECTING | 1991 | citrine | diamonds | gold | platinum

Ring | REFLEKTIERENDE PERSPEKTIVEN | 1993 | Turmalin | Gold | Platin || Ring | REFLECTING PERSPECTIVES | 1993 | tourmaline | gold | platinum

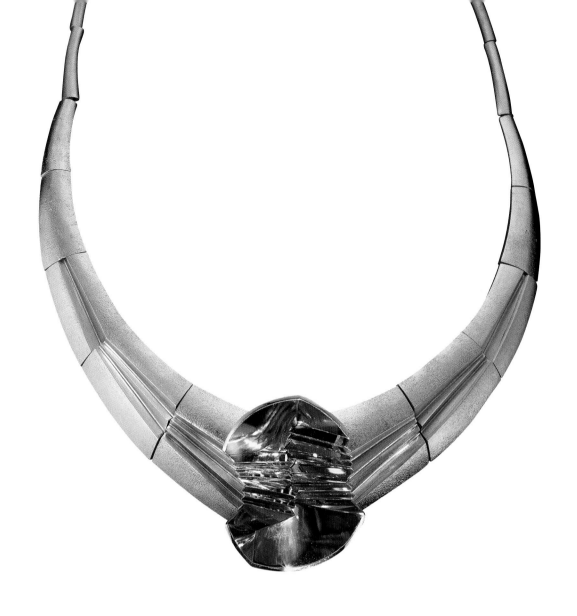

Halsschmuck | REFLEKTIERENDE PERSPEKTIVEN | 1993 | Amethyst/Citrin | Platin | Gold | Michael M. Scott Collection || Neck Jewellery |
REFLECTING PERSPECTIVES | 1993 | amethyst/citrine | platinum | gold | Michael M. Scott Collection

Skulptur | RHYTHMUS | 1991 | Beryll | Platin | H 10 cm || Sculpture | RHYTHM | 1991 | beryl | platinum | H 10 cm

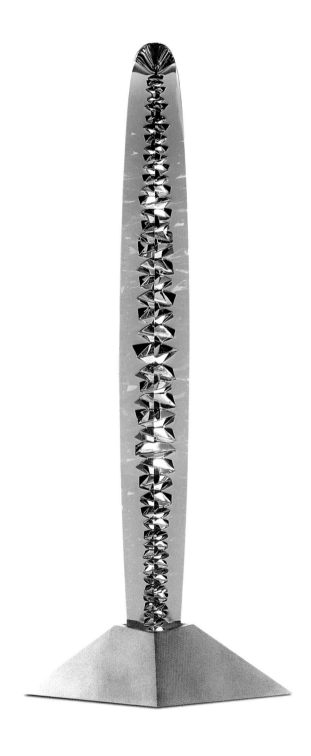

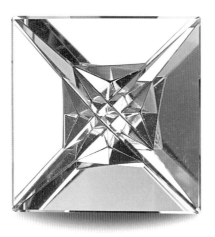

CONTEXT CUT | 1992 | Bergkristall 31,80 ct || CONTEXT CUT | 1992 | rock crystal 31.80 ct

CONTEXT CUT | 1992 | Bergkristall 27,22 ct || CONTEXT CUT | 1992 | rock crystal 27.22 ct

Ring | CONTEXT DIAMOND | 1992 | Platin | Jade || Ring | CONTEXT DIAMOND | 1992 | platinum | jade

Skulptur | LICHTZYKLUS | 1993 | Bergkristall mit Rutil | H 28 cm || Sculpture | LIGHT CYCLE | 1993 | rock crystal with rutile | H 28 cm

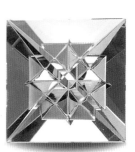

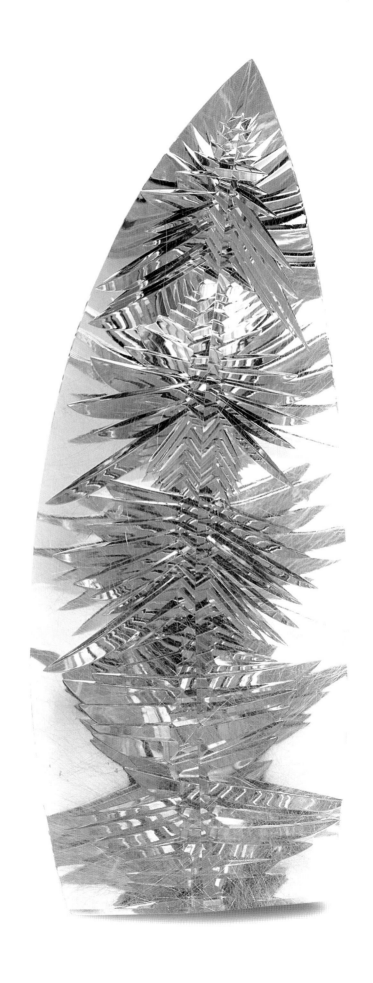

DIE BLAUE VARIANTE DES BERYLL WIRD SEIT DER ANTIKE MIT DEM MEERWASSER IN VERBINDUNG GEBRACHT. »AQUA MARINA« SPIEGELT DEN RHYTHMUS DER GEZEITEN, DEN SCHLAG DER WELLEN. IM MITTELALTER SCHMÜCKTE ER ALS SYMBOL DER KEUSCHHEIT MARIENSTATUEN. »DOM PEDRO«, EIN RIESIGER, KLARER UND FAST MAKELLOSER AQUAMARIN-ROHKRISTALL MIT KNAPP 26 KG GEWICHT WIRD DURCH BERND MUNSTEINER NACH EINEM GENAUEN STUDIUM DER EINSCHLÜSSE, RISSE, SPRÜNGE UND DES FARBENSPIELS ZUM OBELISKEN. AUF DER RÜCKSEITE BRECHEN SICH WELLENFÖRMIG AUFEINANDER ZULAUFENDE EINSCHNITTE: »ONDAS MARITIMAS«.

Kristall | DOM PEDRO | 1993 | Aquamarin 24 875 g | H 59 cm || Crystal | DOM PEDRO | 1993 | aquamarine 24 875 g | H 59 cm

SINCE ANTIQUITY THIS BLUE VARIANT OF BERYL HAS BEEN ASSOCIATED WITH THE WATERS OF THE SEA. ›AQUA MARINA‹ REFLECTS THE RHYTHM OF THE TIDES, THE BREAKING OF WAVES. IN THE MIDDLE AGES AQUAMARINE ADORNED STATUES OF THE VIRGIN AS A SYMBOL OF CHASTITY. ›DOM PEDRO‹, A GIGANTIC, CLEAR, ALMOST FLAWLESS UNCUT AQUAMARINE CRYSTAL WEIGHING ABOUT 26 KG, HAS BECOME AN OBELISK AFTER BERND MUNSTEINER SUBJECTED ITS INCLUSIONS, FISSURES, CRACKS AND THE PLAY OF LIGHT ON AND WITHIN IT TO EXACTING STUDY. ON THE BACK CUTS BREAK LIKE WAVES AGAINST EACH OTHER: ›ONDAS MARITIMAS‹.

Skulptur | DOM PEDRO — ONDAS MARITIMAS | 1993 | Aquamarin | H 35 cm || Sculpture | DOM PEDRO — WAVES ·OF THE SEA | 1993 | aquamarine | H 35 cm

LIGHT IN STONE
Michael M. Scott

After retiring as the first president of Apple Computer, I attended a private art show featuring a variety of artists from the Idar-Oberstein area of Germany, among them Bernd Munsteiner. The uniqueness of each of his pieces still really impresses me. I saw ›Reflecting Perspectives V‹, which was at that time Munsteiner's largest piece. The thirteen inch tall, 7650 ct sculpture was fashioned from a piece of bi-colored smoky quartz with cuts in the back as well as the front. Its base was clear, but it grew darker towards the top. It was the first time I had seen Munsteiner's invention, the now world standard ›fantasy cut.‹ I fell in love with that piece and became the first of many Munsteiner purchases.

There are a lot of things happening in Munsteiner's pieces so that as one shifts their viewpoint the whole pattern of light inside the stone shifts around, revealing new ›scenes‹ within the stones. There are sweet spots to discover in which the piece stunningly blossoms before your eyes. His technique tends to draw the viewer into the stone to see what is going on inside. You can see each piece is unique and memorable on its own.

Traditionally, a cutter would take a lump of rough stone to a flat grinding disc that is used to make the flat faces around the piece. When you turn the stone to different angles the light is reflected off these flat surfaces. What Munsteiner invented was the ›fantasy cut‹ which is a negative cut into the stone. He cuts inward! Polishing the bottom where the two cuts meet is impossible with a traditional grinding wheel. Without a polished meeting of the two cut planes, the cut could look nasty and take away from the piece. Not only has Munsteiner invented the ›fantasy cut‹, he has also had to invent special tools so that he can get into his cut, a guarded trade secret. He's invented the mechanism that allows one to do a whole new type of visual work in this solid medium. I appreciate the mechanics and the science of how he does these, but it's the creative work that is most stunning.

Munsteiner further challenges traditional cutting with matching the cuts in the back of the stone with a couple of small cuts in the front, so that the front and back reflect against each other, adding to the piece's depth

IN STEIN GEBANNTES LICHT
Michael M. Scott

Nachdem ich als erster Präsident von Apple Computer zurückgetreten war, besuchte ich eine private Kunstausstellung, die eine Reihe von Künstlern aus der Region Idar-Oberstein vorstellte, darunter auch Bernd Munsteiner. Die Einzigartigkeit jedes seiner Stücke beeindruckt mich noch immer tief. Ich sah »Reflektierende Perspektiven V«, damals Munsteiners größte Arbeit. Die 33 cm hohe Skulptur mit 7650 Karat aus einem Stück zweifarbigem Rauchquarz war sowohl an der Vorder- als auch an der Rückseite mit Einschnitten versehen. Das untere Ende war klar, aber nach oben hin wurde der Stein dunkler. Es war das erste Mal, dass ich Munsteiners Erfindung sah, den »Fantasy Cut«, der heute Weltstandard erreicht hat. Ich verliebte mich in dieses Stück und kaufte es; weitere Munsteiner-Stücke sollten folgen.

In Munsteiners Arbeiten passiert viel. Wenn man den Blickwinkel wechselt, ändert sich auch das gesamte Lichtmuster im Innern eines Steins und gewährt dem Betrachter ganz neue Einblicke. Man entdeckt interessante Stellen, an denen das Stück auf wunderbare Weise vor den Augen des Betrachters »erblüht«. Munsteiners Technik möchte den Betrachter in den Stein »hineinziehen« – er soll sehen, was dort im Innern vorgeht. So erkennt er, dass jedes Stück einzigartig und auf seine Weise unvergesslich ist.

Traditionell bearbeitete ein Schleifer einen Brocken Rohstein mit einer flachen Schleifscheibe, die flache Facetten rund um den Stein erzeugt. Wenn man den Stein in verschiedenen Winkeln dreht, wird Licht von diesen Flächen reflektiert. Munsteiners Erfindung ist der »Fantasy Cut«, ein negativer Schnitt in den Stein hinein. Er schleift nach innen! Mit einem traditionellen Schleifrad ist es unmöglich, das untere Ende, wo die beiden Schliffe sich treffen, zu glätten. Aber durch ein unsauberes Aufeinandertreffen

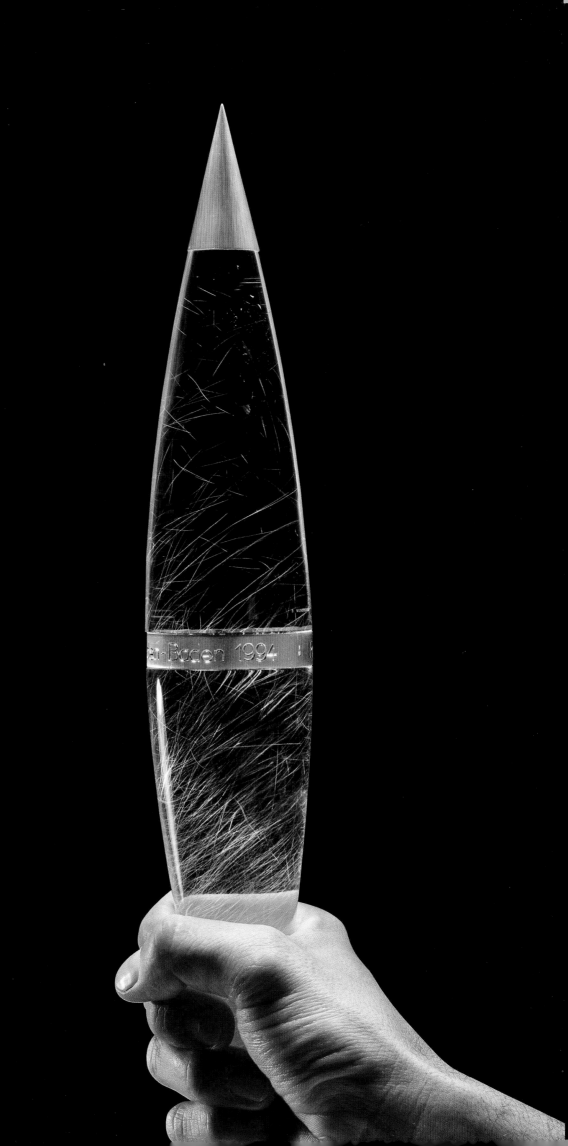

and giving it a more vibrant life. As a third generation artisan, Munsteiner's influence is apparent since his ›fantasy cut‹ is now imitated throughout the world. But the others lack the life and the excitement of an original Munsteiner.

An ›ideal cut‹ is supposed to be the best cut for a diamond. With all of today's technologies, we still don't know how to scientifically cut the faces or the angles in order to get the light just right. To me, Munsteiner has those calculations naturally built into his brain to allow him to set the angles to bring out that sparkle and joy that lies hidden in a raw stone. As Munsteiner says, he first takes the piece and lets it ›talk‹ to him and only after that does he try to ›release‹ the piece. So for me one of the most exciting things about his work is that he knows how to get the different cuts to bring out the brilliance, taking into account that no two stones are alike. Each one requires a different strategy.

After he's made his major cuts Munsteiner looks at the stone and decides what he wants to add. With additional cuts, he risks that the stone shatters. If he goes too far he could ruin the piece.

Because Munsteiner works with such large stones, his risk is even higher. ›Metamorphosis‹, originally a very large boulder, is a good example. After he acquired the stone, he could have cut it into smaller pieces, and potentially made more money. Even though he would have a better chance selling many smaller stones, he took a risk with cutting a very large stone that might have been impossible to sell. He limited his market to not only someone who may buy ›Metamorphosis‹ because it's beautiful, but also to someone who would be willing to spend the extra money that goes with such a large, grand piece.

Another example of his fearlessness is the piece ›Dom Pedro,‹ made from a very large aquamarine crystal. Again, he took a huge stone that could have easily sold as smaller pieces, but he chose to make one large piece, risking that the piece could splinter. He's willing, in a business sense, to take a calculated risk. I have to give him credit for his entrepreneurship as well as his talent in sculpture.

Through the years, Bernd Munsteiner has always worked to reinvent himself. I've witnessed five or six phases,

der beiden Flächen könnte der Schliff leicht unschön wirken, und dies würde die Qualität des Stücks beeinträchtigen. Munsteiner hat nicht nur den »Fantasy Cut« erfunden, er musste auch spezielle Werkzeuge entwickeln, um in die durch seine Einschnitte entstandenen Furchen zu kommen. Er hat eine Vorgehensweise entwickelt, die eine völlig neue Art visueller Arbeit mit diesem festen Material ermöglicht. Wie das funktioniert, ist ein wohlgehütetes Geheimnis. Ich schätze zwar die mechanische und wissenschaftliche Seite seines Schaffens sehr, aber dennoch ist gerade die kreative Arbeit am überwältigendsten.

Munsteiner stellt die traditionelle Schleifkunst außerdem dadurch in Frage, dass er den Schliffen auf der Rückseite des Steins einige kleine Einschliffe auf der Vorderseite gegenüberstellt, so dass die Vorder- und die Rückseite sich gegenseitig spiegeln und das Stück tiefer und lebendiger machen. Munsteiner ist Edelsteinschleifer in der dritten Generation, und sein Einfluss ist offensichtlich, da der »Fantasy Cut« heute auf der ganzen Welt nachgeahmt wird. Aber die anderen sind nicht so lebendig und aufregend wie ein echter Munsteiner.

Ein »Idealschliff« sollte eigentlich der beste Schliff für einen Diamanten sein. Trotz all der technologischen Mittel von heute wissen wir aber immer noch nicht, wie man die Oberflächen oder Kanten so schleift, dass das Licht genau richtig einfällt. Meiner Meinung nach sind diese wissenschaftlichen Berechnungen ganz natürlich in Munsteiners Kopf vorhanden. Sie erlauben ihm, die Ecken und Kanten genau so zu setzen, dass der in einem Rohstein verborgene Funke entfacht wird. Wie Munsteiner selbst sagt, nimmt er zuerst das Stück und lässt es zu sich sprechen, und erst danach versucht er, das Stück zu »befreien«. Die Tatsache, dass er weiß, wie man durch verschiedene Schleifarten diese Brillanz zum Vorschein bringt, ist in meinen Augen einer der aufregendsten Aspekte seiner Arbeit. Dabei berücksichtigt er, dass kein Stein wie der andere ist. Jeder verlangt eine andere Strategie.

Nachdem er die ersten großen Schnitte gemacht hat, schaut sich Munsteiner den Stein in Ruhe an und entscheidet, was er noch hinzufügen möchte. Durch zusätzliche

Schliffe geht er das Risiko ein, dass der Stein zerbricht. Wenn er zu weit geht, könnte er das Stück sogar zerstören.

Weil Munsteiner mit so großen Steinen arbeitet, ist sein Risiko sogar noch größer. Das Stück »Metamorphose«, ursprünglich ein riesiger Steinbrocken, ist ein gutes Beispiel. Nachdem er den Stein erstanden hatte, hätte er ihn in kleinere Stücke zerteilen können, und damit gewiss mehr Geld verdient. Aber obwohl er mehr Chancen gehabt hätte, viele kleine Steine zu verkaufen, ging er das Risiko ein, einen sehr großen, möglicherweise unverkäuflichen Stein zu bearbeiten. Er beschränkte damit seinen Markt nicht nur auf den Kundenkreis, der die Skulptur »Metamorphose« kauft, weil sie schön ist, sondern auch auf die Käufer, die bereit sind, für ein so großes und wundervolles Stück sehr viel Geld auszugeben.

Ein weiteres Beispiel für Munsteiners Furchtlosigkeit ist die Arbeit »Dom Pedro« aus einem sehr großen Aquamarinkristall. Erneut verwendete er hier einen riesigen Stein, der sich in kleineren Stücken spielend verkauft hätte, entschloss sich aber, eine einzelne, große Arbeit daraus zu machen und riskierte, dass der Stein zersplitterte. Betriebswirtschaftlich gesprochen, ist er bereit, ein kalkuliertes Risiko einzugehen. Sowohl für seinen Unternehmergeist als auch für sein Talent als Bildhauer gilt ihm daher meine Anerkennung.

All die Jahre hat Bernd Munsteiner immer daran gearbeitet, sich selbst neu zu erfinden. Ich habe fünf oder sechs Phasen miterlebt, von seinen frühen flachen Achatreliefs über seine erotische Serie bis hin zum Gebrauch von Laser-Fräsmaschinen für Materialien, in die er seine Steine präzise einsetzen konnte. Ich hatte das große Glück, die Entwicklung seiner Arbeit über die Jahre hinweg verfolgen zu können. Ich weiß, dass er immer noch versucht, einen Stein zu finden, der ihm ein noch größeres Werk als bisher ermöglicht. »Metamorphose« ist der größte facettierte Edelstein der Welt, aber das genügt ihm nicht. Mit ein wenig Glück wird er noch Gewaltigeres schaffen.

from his early flat panels to his erotica series to his use of laser milling machines for materials in which to precision set his stones. I've been very lucky to watch his work evolve over time. I know that he still wants to find some material that allows him to make an even larger work than anything he's done. ›Metamorphosis‹ is the largest faceted gemstone in the world, but for him, that's not enough. With luck, he will do something grander still.

Skulptur | SYMBOLON | 1994 | Bergkristall mit Rutil || Sculpture | SYMBOLON | 1994 | rock crystal with rutile

Halsschmuck | SYMBOLON | 1994 | Bergkristall mit Rutil || Neck jewellery | SYMBOLON | 1994 | rock crystal with rutile

Skulptur | SYMBOLON | 1995 | Morganit | Michael M. Scott Collection || Sculpture | SYMBOLON | 1995 | morganite | Michael M. Scott Collection

SYMBOLON | 1995 | Citrin 25,25 ct || SYMBOLON | 1995 | citrine 25.25 ct

Skulptur | SYMBOLON | 1997 | Bergkristall mit Rutil || Sculpture | SYMBOLON | 1997 | rock crystal with rutile

Halsschmuck | SYMBOLON | 1995 | Citrin || Neck jewellery | SYMBOLON | 1995 | citrine

Ring | SYMBOLON | 1997 | Turmalin | Gold || Ring | SYMBOLON | 1997 | tourmaline | gold

Halsschmuck | REFLEKTIERENDE PERSPEKTIVEN | 1994 | Turmalin | Gold | Achatrelief | Michael M. Scott Collection || Neck jewellery | REFLECTING PERSPECTIVES | 1994 | tourmaline | gold | agate relief | Michael M. Scott Collection

Brosche | INSIDE SELECTING | 1994 | Amethyst/Citrin | Gold || Brooch | INSIDE SELECTING | 1994 | amethyst/citrine | gold

Skulptur/Halsschmuck | REFLEKTIERENDE PERSPEKTIVEN | 1994 | Turmalin | Onyxrelief | Spirit Diamond | Platin | Gold | Silber | Bergkristall mit Rutil | Michael M. Scott Collection || Sculpture/Neck jewellery | REFLECTING PERSPECTIVES | 1994 | tourmaline | onyx relief | Spirit Diamond | platinum | gold | silver | rock crystal with rutile | Michael M. Scott Collection

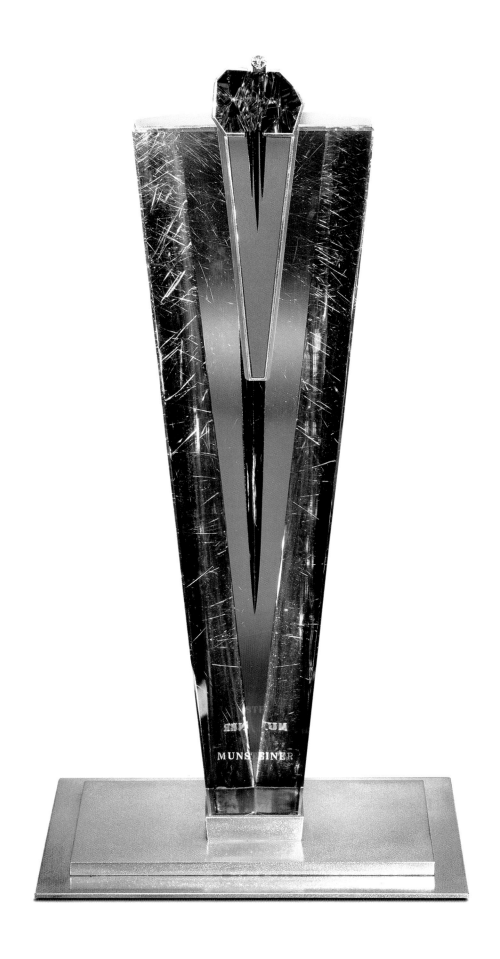

Skulptur | DOM PEDRO – INSIDE SELECTING | 1994 | Aquamarin | Platin || Sculpture | DOM PEDRO – INSIDE SELECTING | 1994 | aquamarine | platinum

Skulptur | DOM PEDRO | 1994 | Aquamarin | Bergkristall | Platin || Sculpture | DOM PEDRO | 1994 | aquamarine | rock crystal | platinum

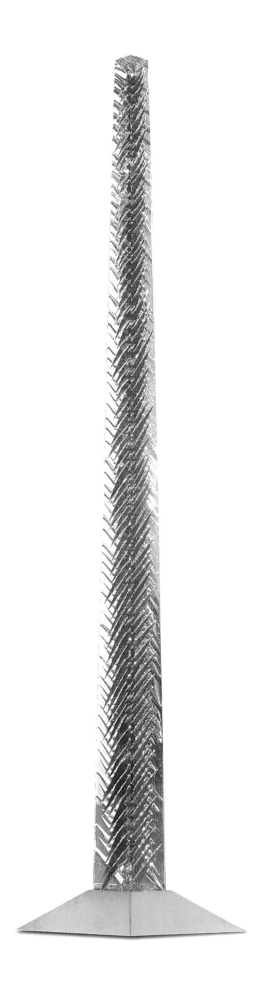

Skulptur | METAMORPHOSE III | 1995 | Bergkristall mit Rutil | Silber || Sculpture | METAMORPHOSIS III | 1995 | rock crystal with rutile | silver

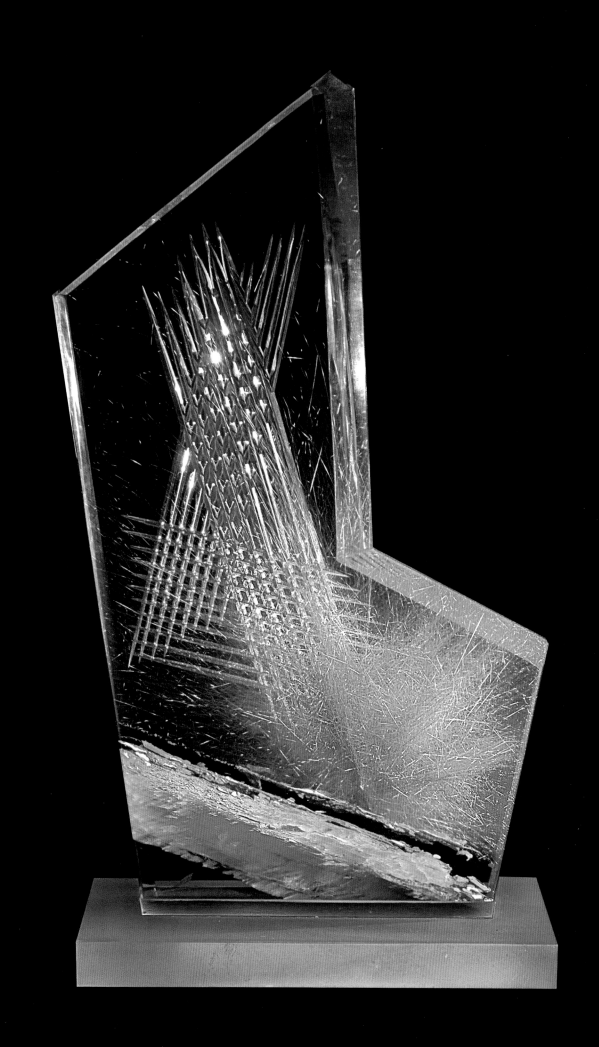

Skulptur | RHYTHMUS I | 1994 | Aquamarin | Platin | Michael M. Scott Collection || Sculpture | RHYTHM I | 1994 | aquamarine | platinum | Michael M. Scott Collection

Skulptur | DOM PEDRO – RHYTHMUS | 1995 | Aquamarin | Platin || Sculpture | DOM PEDRO – RHYTHM | 1995 | aquamarine | platinum

1994–1997

Skulptur/Brosche | REFLEKTIERENDE PERSPEKTIVEN | 1995 | Turmalin | Bergkristall mit Turmalin | Gold | Michael M. Scott Collection ||
Sculpture/Brooch | REFLECTING PERSPECTIVES | 1995 | tourmaline | rock crystal with tourmaline | gold | Michael M. Scott Collection

Objekt/Brosche/Halsschmuck | REFLEKTIERENDE PERSPEKTIVEN | 1995 | Aquamarin | Platin | Gold | Michael M. Scott Collection ||
Object/Brooch/Neck jewellery | REFLECTING PERSPECTIVES | 1995 | aquamarine | platinum | gold | Michael M. Scott Collection

Halsschmuck | D O M P E D R O | 1996 | Aquamarin | Platin || Neck jewellery | D O M P E D R O | 1996 | aquamarine | platinum

Ring | D O M P E D R O | 1996 | Aquamarin | Platin | Gold || Ring | D O M P E D R O | 1996 | aquamarine | platinum | gold

Skulptur | REFLEKTIERENDE PERSPEKTIVEN | 1996 | Turmalin | Bergkristall mit Rutil | Gold | Michael M. Scott Collection || Sculpture | REFLECTING PERSPECTIVES | 1996 | tourmaline | rock crystal with rutile | gold | Michael M. Scott Collection

Drei Objekte | REFLEKTIERENDE PERSPEKTIVEN | 1996 | Beryll | Turmalin | Aquamarin | Gold | Silber | Platin | Achatrelief | Michael M. Scott Collection || Three objects | REFLECTING PERSPECTIVES | 1996 | beryl | tourmaline | aquamarine | gold | silver | platinum | agate relief | Michael M. Scott Collection

Ring | SPIRIT DIAMOND | 1994 | Jade | Platin || Ring | SPIRIT DIAMOND | 1994 | jade | platinum

Ring | CONTEXT DIAMOND | 1997 | Gold | Platin | Schmuckgestaltung: Jutta Munsteiner || Ring | CONTEXT DIAMOND | 1997 | gold | platinum | Jewellery design: Jutta Munsteiner

Ring | CONTEXT CUT | 1995 | Aquamarin | Jade | Platin || Ring | CONTEXT CUT | 1995 | aquamarine | jade | platinum

Ring | SPIRIT DIAMOND | 1994 | Platin | Schmuckgestaltung: Jörg Munsteiner || Ring | SPIRIT DIAMOND | 1994 | platinum | Jewellery design: Jörg Munsteiner

Ring | SPIRIT SUN | 1997 | Peridot | Achatrelief | Gold | Schmuckgestaltung: Tom Munsteiner || Ring | SPIRIT SUN | 1997 | peridot | agate relief |
gold | Jewellery design: Tom Munsteiner

Halsschmuck | EROTIK | 1995 | Citrin | Gold | Platin || Neck jewellery | EROTICISM | 1995 | citrine | gold | platinum

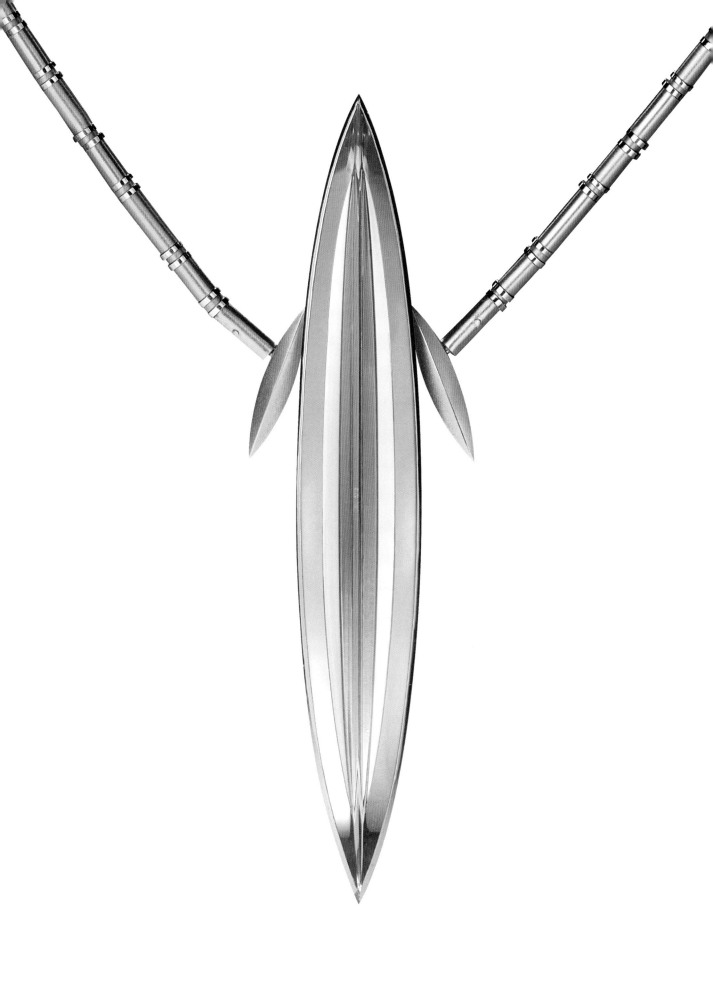

REFLEKTIERENDE PERSPEKTIVEN | 1996 | Turmalin 6,68 ct ‖ REFLECTING PERSPECTIVES | 1996 | tourmaline 6.68 ct

REFLEKTIERENDE PERSPEKTIVEN | 1995 | Peridot 49,33 ct ‖ REFLECTING PERSPECTIVES | 1995 | peridot 49.33 ct

REFLEKTIERENDE PERSPEKTIVEN | 1994 | Aquamarin 25,27 ct ‖ REFLECTING PERSPECTIVES | 1994 | aquamarine 25.27 ct

REFLEKTIERENDE PERSPEKTIVEN | 1996 | Turmalin 45,63 ct ‖ REFLECTING PERSPECTIVES | 1996 | tourmaline 45.63 ct

REFLEKTIERENDE PERSPEKTIVEN | 1997 | Aquamarin 17,65 ct || REFLECTING PERSPECTIVES | 1997 | aquamarine 17.65 ct

REFLEKTIERENDE PERSPEKTIVEN | 1997 | Turmalin 21,61 ct || REFLECTING PERSPECTIVES | 1997 | tourmaline 21.61 ct

REFLEKTIERENDE PERSPEKTIVEN | 1997 | Morganit 62,01 ct || REFLECTING PERSPECTIVES | 1997 | morganite 62.01 ct

ZUM KRISTALL ERSTARRTES GESTEIN, VER-
STEINERTES EIS NACH ANTIKER VORSTELLUNG,
VERWEIST AUF DAS ENDE VON BEWEGUNG
UND ZEITLICHKEIT. MUNSTEINERS IN
SPANNUNGSREICHEN VERLÄUFEN RHYTHMISCH
GETAKTETE EINSCHNITTE SPÜREN ALS
POETISCHE ZEUGEN DEM PULSSCHLAG DER
NATÜRLICHEN KRISTALLISATION, DEN
DYNAMISCHEN KRÄFTEN UND TEKTONISCHEN
GEWALTEN IM ENTSTEHUNGSPROZESS DER
ERDE NACH.

CRYSTALLISED STONE, PETRIFIED ICE AS
ANTIQUITY BELIEVED, REFERS TO THE END OF
MOVEMENT AND THIS LIFE ON EARTH.
MUNSTEINER'S CUTS, PLACED TO MEASURE
AN EXCITING RHYTHM, TAKE THE PULSE OF
NATURAL CRYSTALLISATION, BEARING POETIC
WITNESS TO THE DYNAMIC POWERS AND
TECTONIC FORCES AT PLAY WHEN THE EARTH
WAS IN THE PROCESS OF BEING FORMED.

Bild | KRISTALL–REFLEXIONEN | 1998 | Bergkristall mit Rutil | Aluminium | Stahl || Picture | CRYSTAL REFLECTIONS | 1998 | rock crystal with rutile | aluminium | steel

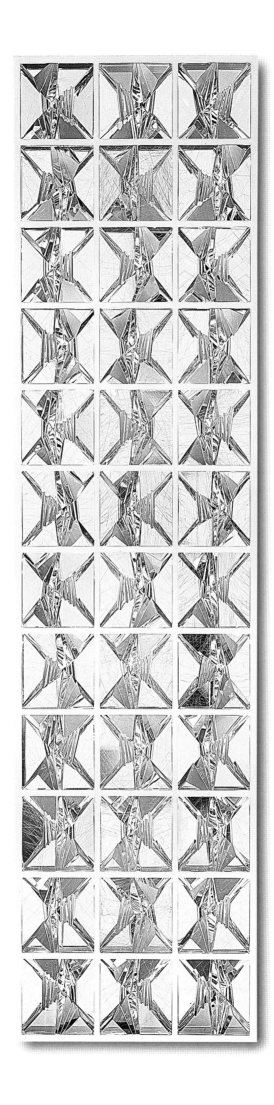

Bild | MILLENNIUM–KRISTALL–REFLEXIONEN | 2000 | Bergkristall | Rauchquarz | Citrin | Aluminium | Stahl | Picture | MILLENNIUM CRYSTAL REFLECTIONS | 2000 | rock crystal | smoky quartz | citrine | aluminium | steel

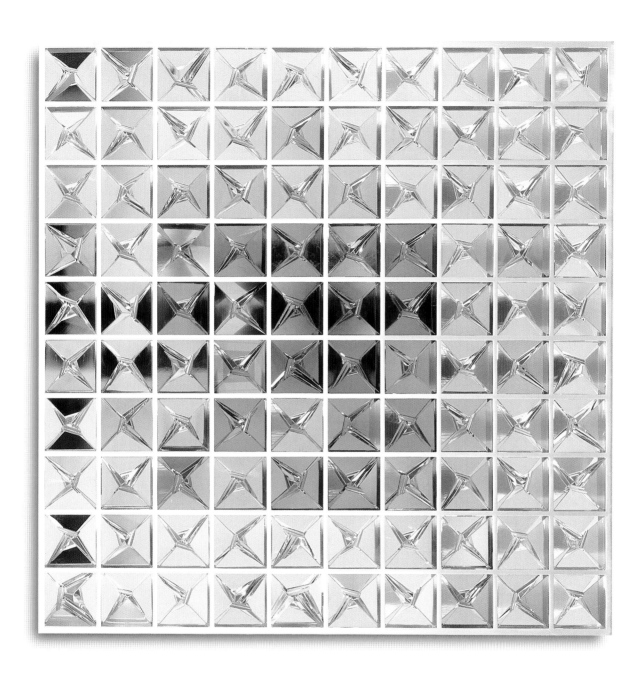

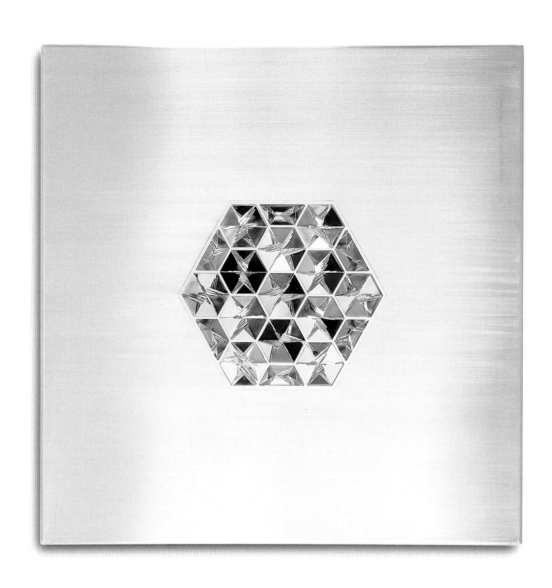

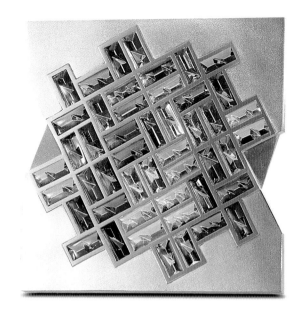

Bild | KRISTALL-REFLEXIONEN | 2002 | Citrin | Aluminium | Stahl || Picture | CRYSTAL REFLECTIONS | 2002 | citrine | aluminium | steel

Halsschmuck | KRISTALL-REFLEXIONEN | 2002 | Turmalin | Peridot | Aquamarin | Goldberyll | Gold || Neck jewellery | CRYSTAL REFLECTIONS | 2002 | tourmaline | peridot | aquamarine | golden beryl | gold

Halsschmuck | KRISTALL-REFLEXIONEN | 2002 | Turmalin | Gold || Neck jewellery | CRYSTAL REFLECTIONS | 2002 | tourmaline | gold

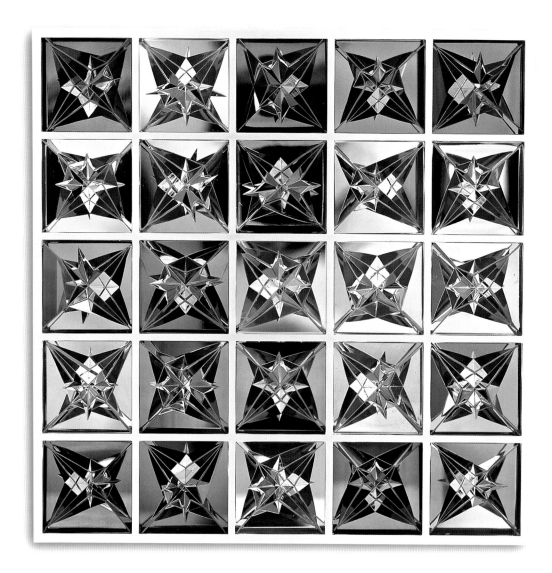

Bild | KRISTALL−REFLEXIONEN | 1999 | Rauchquarz | Citrin | Aluminium | Stahl || Picture | CRYSTAL REFLECTIONS | 1999 | smoky quartz | citrine | aluminium | steel

Bild/Brosche | MORGANIT−REFLEXIONEN | 1998 | Morganit | Gold | Stahl || Picture/Brooch | MORGANITE REFLECTIONS | 1998 | morganite | gold | steel

Bild/Brosche | TURMALIN−REFEXIONEN | 2001 | Turmalin | Gold | Stahl || Picture/Brooch | TOURMALINE REFLECTIONS | 2001 | tourmaline | gold | steel

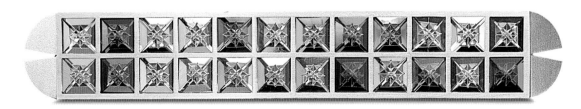

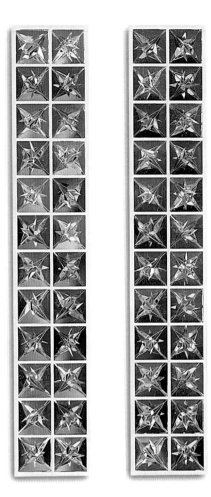

Bild | KRISTALL–REFLEXIONEN | 2002 | Bergkristall mit Rutil || Picture | CRYSTAL REFLECTIONS | 2002 | rock crystal with rutile

DEBORAH AQUADO

BERNDS ARBEITEN

Deborah Aquado

Es ist für mich eine ehrenvolle und zugleich nicht ganz einfache Aufgabe, über Bernd Munsteiners Werk zu schreiben und darüber, was es für mich bedeutet. Ich hatte in den frühen 1970er Jahren von Idar-Oberstein, der Stadt der Edelsteine, gehört. 1974 ging ich nach meinem Sommerkurs in Salzburg für ein paar Tage dorthin. Allerdings wagte ich mich damals nicht aus Oberstein heraus. Wenn es regnete, schien es der dunkelste Platz der Welt zu sein, vielleicht weil das, was folgte, in so starkem Kontrast dazu stand. Sobald ich nämlich nach Idar, Tiefenstein, Kirschweiler und Stipshausen fuhr, wurde das Land freundlicher und auch meine Stimmung hellte sich auf. Da ich mich an einen Artikel über Bernd Munsteiners Arbeit in der *Goldschmiedezeitung* erinnerte, fuhr ich nach Stipshausen, um ihn ausfindig zu machen. Mein erstes Treffen mit der Familie Munsteiner war bedeutsam, und die Steine waren überwältigender als ich erwartet hatte. Ich fühlte mich schwach und schwindelig, da ich sie gar nicht alle auf einen Blick wahrnehmen konnte – vielmehr brauchte ich Zeit, um jeden einzelnen Stein genau zu betrachten und zu untersuchen.

Mit großer Faszination kam ich immer wieder immer wieder nach Stipshausen, Idar-Oberstein und zur Edelsteinstraße zurück und begann, Bernd Munsteiners Steine zu kaufen und damit zu experimentieren. Es war ein ziemliches Erlebnis, meinen eigenen Weg im Umgang mit seinen Steinen zu finden, die ihren ganz eigenen, intensiven Charakter haben, vor dem man unbedingt Respekt haben sollte. Ich wollte, dass meine Metallarbeiten die visuellen Erscheinungen des Edelsteinschliffs fortsetzten. Als sich meine Arbeit weiterentwickelte, wurden andere Phänomene im Innern der Steine zu neuen Herausforderungen.

Munsteiner führte in den späten 1970er Jahren regelmäßige Ausstellungen in seiner Werkstatt-Galerie ein, die im Zwei-Jahres-Rhythmus stattfanden. 1982 wurden

BERND'S WORK

Deborah Aquado

It is daunting to write of Bernd Munsteiner's work, and what it means to my world. I'd heard of Idar-Oberstein, city of stones, in the early 1970s. In 1974, after my summer workshop in Salzburg, I went there for a few days and didn't venture out of Oberstein at that time. It seemed to be the darkest place when it rains than anywhere else in the world, perhaps because what followed contrasted so. I ventured out into Idar, Tiefenstein, Kirschweiler, and Stipshausen, the land became friendlier, my mood lightened, and the memory of an article in the *Goldschmiede-Zeitung* of Bernd Munsteiner's work was propelling me to Stipshausen to find him. My first meeting with the Munsteiner family was momentous, and the stones were much more than anticipated. I was weak and dizzy – one could not absorb them in a glance – each stone took its time for your scrutiny and contemplation.

I returned to Stipshausen, Idar-Oberstein, and the *Edelsteinstrasse* with great fascination, and I began to purchase and experiment with Bernd Munsteiner's stones. It was quite an experience to find my own way with his stones. They are objects of intense and specific character that must be reckoned with. I wanted my metalwork to continue the visual phenomena created by the cutting of the stone. As my work progressed, other phenomena, internal to the stone, challenged me further.

Munsteiner launched a tradition of bi-annual exhibitions at his studio-gallery in the late 1970s. The exhibition of my work at the gallery was in 1982. The exhibitions were group, fastidiously curated with stunning work shown. The best jewelry, best gemstones, sculpture, ceramics, and painting were the frequent media presented. Preparations for the Munsteiners' exhibitions involved fastidious and very hard work, inventorying, pricing, and cataloging, all in one day, as the artists and their work usually arrived simultaneously. Arrivals usually occurred on Thursday morning for the exhibition's opening on Friday evening.

Tom Munsteiner, Bernd's son, and I challenged each other to decide which evening's dinner was the best. As each exhibition was a weekend-long event, Friday was the official opening with celebrations of the new work that most of the guests had never seen before. This was the excitement, the energy of the opening, beautiful people wearing beautiful contemporary jewelry, new people, old friends, distinguished introductions, the highest energy, the food and great wine presented, familiar and warmly delicious. The contrast of ›opulence‹ and ›rusticity‹ was so evident, champagne and würstels, pretzels, and schmaltz, and everyone commenting to each other (in all languages) that we simply do not eat this way – that is at any other time except here at the Munsteiners'.

At my exhibition in 1982, I remember the huge pretzels hanging from the studio ceiling – 18 to 20 feet high on ropes with wooden toggles holding them on – elegant and high columns of pretzels – you tore off a piece and the column got shorter. Remembered also, the bottle of ›Scharzhofberg‹ that was too large to fit through the door, and after that, I could never stay away. We would then proceed to ›Zum Dicke Hennes‹ for *Spiessbraten*, the chosen entertainment, celebrating until very late. Saturday night, dinner at the ›Schlossmühle,‹ with exquisite food, more ›haute‹ than the night before. Great wine

and more and more ebullient celebrations. Tom and I decided Fridays were the best.

Our specific group of international studio goldsmiths grew and grew as Bernd's work became more widely known. Language notwithstanding, our knowledge of each other and of Munsteiner's work intensified. Recognition by the jewelry and gemstone industry joined the studio jewelry community in enormous appreciation of his work. He reached successfully between industry and art as never before in this field. The bi-annual exhibitions at the Munsteiner gallery in Stipshausen was an important component of his reach. In the studio jewelry community, the exhibitions became more and more exciting as his own new work was featured. Our enthusiasm for his work was brought back to our respective communities across Europe and North America, from Greece to New York City, and his work grew, matured, increased in volume and in dimension.

Bernd, Hanne, their son Tom and his wife Jutta continue the family business. Tom, also a gemstone cutter, creates work that is exquisite, although quite distinct from his father's, and collaborates with his wife Jutta's wonder-

meine Arbeiten präsentiert. Es waren anspruchsvoll kuratierte Gruppenausstellungen, die großartige Stücke zeigten. Das Spektrum reichte von bestem Schmuck und besten Edelsteinen über Bildhauerei und Keramik bis hin zur Malerei. Die Vorbereitungen für die Ausstellung bei den Munsteiners war mit anspruchsvoller und sehr harter Arbeit verbunden: Inventarisierung, Bewertung der Preise und Katalogisierung, und das alles an einem einzigen Tag, da die Künstler und ihre Werke für gewöhnlich zusammen eintrafen. Sie kamen normalerweise Donnerstag morgens an, die Ausstellung wurde Freitag abends eröffnet.

Tom Munsteiner, Bernds Sohn, und ich stellten uns die Frage, an welchem Abend das Essen wohl am besten sei. Da jede Ausstellung ein Wochenende lang dauerte, war freitags die offizielle Eröffnung. Die neuen Werke, die die meisten Gäste noch nie zuvor gesehen hatten, wurden gefeiert. Da war diese Aufregung, die Energie der Eröffnung, schöne Menschen, die schönen zeitgenössischen Schmuck trugen, neue Leute, alte Freunde, bedeutende Begegnungen, das Essen und der hervorragende Wein, vertraut, warm und köstlich. Der Kontrast zwischen »Opulenz« und »Rustikalität« war offensichtlich: Champagner und Würstchen, Brezeln und Schmalz. Wir Gäste sagten zueinander (in allen möglichen Sprachen), dass wir sonst einfach andere Essgewohnheiten hätten – nur hier bei den Munsteiners aßen wir so… Ich erinnere mich an die riesigen Brezeln, die bei meiner Ausstellung 1982 von der Decke der Werkstatt hingen – 5 bis 6 Meter hoch an Seilen mit hölzernen Halterungen. Es gab auch elegante, hohe Säulen aus Brezeln – man riss ein Stück ab und die Säule wurde kürzer. Ich erinnere mich außerdem an die Flasche »Scharzhofberg«, die nicht durch die Türe passte, weil sie zu groß war – aber danach konnte ich nicht mehr davon lassen. Wir gingen dann zum »Dicke Hennes«, um Spießbraten zu essen und bis in den frühen Morgen zu feiern. Samstag nachts Abendessen in der »Schlossmühle«, mit erlesenen Speisen, mehr *haute cuisine* als die Nacht zuvor. Großartiger Wein und zunehmend überschwängliches Feiern. Tom und ich beschlossen, dass die Freitage am besten waren.

DEBORAH AQUADO

Als Bernds Arbeit immer bekannter wurde, vergrößerte sich auch unsere spezielle Gruppe internationaler Goldschmiede, die mit Bernds Atelier in Verbindung standen. Trotz der Sprachbarrieren intensivierte sich unser Wissen über die anderen und über Munsteiners Werk. Neben der enormen Wertschätzung durch diese Schmuckwerkstatt-Gemeinschaft zollte nun auch die Schmuck- und Edelsteinindustrie seiner Arbeit Anerkennung. Wie niemand zuvor in diesem Bereich baute er erfolgreich eine Brücke zwischen Industrie und Kunst. Die jedes zweite Jahr stattfindenden Ausstellungen in der Munsteiner-Galerie in Stipshausen waren wichtiger Bestandteil dieser Brücke. Für die Schmuckwerkstatt-Gemeinschaft wurden die Ausstellungen immer interessanter, da dort nun auch seine eigenen neuen Arbeiten vorgestellt wurden. Unsere Begeisterung für sein Werk strahlte bis in unsere jeweiligen Gemeinschaften in ganz Europa und Nordamerika hinein, von Griechenland bis New York City, während seine Arbeit wuchs, reifte und an Volumen und Dimension zunahm.

Bernd, Hanne, ihr Sohn Tom und dessen Frau Jutta führen heute das Familien-unternehmen fort. Tom, selbst Edelsteinschleifer, kreiert außerordentliche Arbeiten, die sich allerdings deutlich von denen seines Vaters unterscheiden, und arbeitet auch mit den wunderbaren Metall-Arbeiten seiner Frau Jutta. Der andere, inzwischen verstorbene Sohn, Jörg, schuf wunderschönen Schmuck aus Bernds und Toms besten Steinen.

Für Bernd selbst hat die Interaktion mit den erstaunlichsten Gebilden, die unser Planet hervorbringt, in einem solchen organischen Prozess eine neue Sprache, ein seine Arbeit beschreibendes Hilfsmittel, erforderlich gemacht. »Inside Selecting«, »Metamorphose« und »Reflektierende Perspektiven« sind nur einige Beispiele. Für mich sind diese Titel Wegweiser dahin, wo er war, als er in das Material eintauchte, etwas abtrug, um etwas anderes freizulegen und entschied, was er wegnehmen wollte.

Was unsere Generation miterleben durfte, nämlich das Entstehen von Bernd Munsteiners Werk, ist bedeutend, historisch bedeutend, und noch nie zuvor da gewesen.

ful work in metal. Another son Jörg, now deceased, produced beautiful jewelry utilizing the best stones of Bernd and Tom.

For Bernd himself, in this organic process, his interaction with the most amazing products of our planet has thus necessitated this creation of a new language, a descriptive handle, referring to his process with each event, experience or series. ›Inside Selecting,‹ ›Metamorphosis,‹ and ›Reflective Perspectives‹ are a few. For me, the titles are his physical guides to where he was, diving into the material, removing to uncover, and selecting what to take away.

What has happened to us in this generation, with the advent of Bernd Munsteiner's work, is momentous, historically so, and has never been experienced before.

Tür eines Wohnhauses | KRISTALL–REFLEXIONEN | 2001 | Schott–Glas | House door | CRYSTAL REFLECTIONS | 2001 | Schott glass

Skulptur | BLUE QUARTZ MILLENNIUM | 1999 | blauer Quarz | Standort: GIA | Gemmological Institute of America | The Robert Mouawad Campus | Carlsbad | Kalifornien/USA | Sponsor: Julius Sauer | Rio de Janeiro/BR || Sculpture | BLUE QUARTZ MILLENNIUM | 1999 | blue quartz | Location: GIA Gemmological Institute of America | The Robert Mouawad Campus | Carlsbad | California/USA | Sponsor: Julius Sauer | Rio de Janeiro/BR

Skulpturen | SCHMERLEBACH UND STEBESHUSEN | 1998 | Kuselit-Vulkanit | Standort: Unter den zwei Linden | Stipshausen/D || Sculptures |
SCHMERLEBACH AND STEBESHUSEN | 1998 | Kuselite-Vulcanite | Location: Unter den zwei Linden | Stipshausen/D

Skulptur | DREI PHASEN | 2002 | Kuselit-Vulkanit | Standort: Skulpturenpark | Stipshausen/D || Sculpture | THREE PHASES | 2002 | Kuselite-
Vulcanite | Location: Sculpture Park | Stipshausen/D

Ring | REFLEKTIERENDE PERSPEKTIVEN | 1998 | Spessartin | Platin | Gold || Ring | REFLECTING PERSPECTIVES | 1998 | spessartine | platinum | gold

REFLEKTIERENDE PERSPEKTIVEN | 1999 | Goldberyll 93,32 ct || REFLECTING PERSPECTIVES | 1999 | golden beryl 93.32 ct

Ring | REFLEKTIERENDE PERSPEKTIVEN | 2001 | Aquamarin | Turmalin | Platin | Schmuckgestaltung: Jörg Munsteiner || Ring | REFLECTING PERSPECTIVES | 2001 | aquamarine | tourmaline | platinum | Jewellery design: Jörg Munsteiner

Ring | REFLEKTIERENDE PERSPEKTIVEN | 2003 | Turmalin | Paraiba-Turmalin | Platin | Schmuckgestaltung: Jörg Munsteiner | Michael M. Scott Collection || Ring | REFLECTING PERSPECTIVES | 2003 | tourmaline | Paraiba tourmaline | platinum | Jewellery design: Jörg Munsteiner | Michael M. Scott Collection

Halsschmuck | SYMBOLON | 2002 | Bergkristall mit Rutil | Neck jewellery | SYMBOLON | 2002 | rock crystal with rutile

Halsschmuck | SYMBOLONS | 2003 | Bergkristall mit Rutil | Neck jewellery | SYMBOLONS | 2003 | rock crystal with rutile

BERND MUNSTEINER
UND SEINE WELT DER KRISTALLE

BERND MUNSTEINER
AND HIS WORLD OF CRYSTALS

Christianne Weber-Stöber

»Schon in den literarischen Quellen menschlicher Frühkultur begegnen wir den Edelsteinen. Das Geheimnis dieser zauberschönen Gebilde der Erdentiefe, ihre Härte, Seltenheit, ihre rätselhaften kristallinischen Formen, ihr märchenhaftes Farbenspiel hat zu allen Zeiten das Denken und Wünschen der Völker jedweder Kulturstufe in ihren Bann geschlagen«.[1] Der Autor formuliert hier treffend, was in unzähligen Schriften und Abhandlungen, in ausschweifenden und blumenreichen Geschichten, in Sagen, Märchen und Gedichten von Poeten, Philosophen, Schriftstellern und vielen anderen, die sich dazu berufen fühlten, immer wieder zum Ausdruck gebracht wurde. Die Kulturvölker des Altertums beschäftigen sich vorwiegend mit der weltanschaulich-magischen Bewertung der Edelsteine, ab dem späten Mittelalter beginnt man, sich mit dem Edelstein als mineralogischem Material auseinander zu setzen. Er ist in der *Göttlichen Komödie* von Dante (1265–1321) zu finden, und der Naturforscher und Philosoph Paracelsus (1493–1541) bezeichnet ihn als die »höchste Subtilität der Natur«. Goethe (1749–1832) spricht von der »Seele und dem Zauber der Edelsteine«.

Im Laufe der Zeit gewinnen die Beständigkeit und der materielle Wert des Edelsteins immer mehr an Bedeutung, der »messbare Wert« seiner Reinheit lassen das in der Natur geborgene Mineral zu einem der begehrtesten Güter werden. Der Edelstein wird zum Unterpfand der Liebe, zum Objekt der Begierde – und nicht selten stürzt er seine Besitzer ins Unglück. Berühmte Diamanten wie der »Hope-Diamant« (44,50 ct) oder der »Tiffany-Diamant« (128,51 ct), aber auch zahlreiche andere Edelsteine, wie der »Edward-Rubin« (167 ct) im British Museum of Natural History in London oder der größte geschliffene Sternsaphir, der »Stern von Indien« (536 ct) im American Museum of Natural History in New York, haben Geschichte geschrieben.

Zu Anfang des 20. Jahrhunderts beginnt die Beschäftigung mit der kristallinen Struktur des Edelsteins in Architektur und Kunst. Sie wird zu einem maßgeblichen Kriterium, zu einem neuen »Formgesetz«. Der ewig gültige »Mythos vom Edelstein« wird durch den neuen »Mythos des Kristalls« abgelöst. Die Architekten des Expressionismus

›Gemstones are encountered even in literary sources from early civilisations. The mystique of these enchantingly beautiful formations from the depths of the earth, their hardness, their rarity, their enigmatic crystalline forms, their fairy-tale play of colour, has captured the thoughts and wishes of peoples in all stages of cultural development.‹[1] The author has here aptly put what has been expressed time and time again in innumerable writings and treatises, in verbose stories written in flowery language, in legends, fairy-tales and poems by poets, philosophers, men of letters and all those many others who have felt called upon to do so. Ancient civilisations primarily valued gemstones in terms of their world-view and for the magical properties ascribed to them. From the late Middle Ages people began to study gemstones mineralogically as material. Encountered in Dante's (1265–1321) *Divine Comedy*, they are called by the Swiss physician and philosopher Paracelsus (1493–1541) ›the most sublime subtlety of nature‹. Goethe (1749–1832) speaks of the ›soul and the enchantment of gemstones‹.

Over the centuries the durability and the extrinsic value of gemstones gained in importance. Measured by the standard of ›purity‹, the mineral concealed in nature's bosom evolved into the most sought-after of all worldly goods. Gemstones became the pledge of security in love and were themselves coveted as objects – and not infrequently they have brought misfortune to their owners. Celebrated diamonds such as the ›Hope Diamond‹ (44.50 ct) and the ›Tiffany Diamond‹ (128.51 ct) in company with numerous other precious stones, including the ›Edward Ruby‹ (167 ct) in the British Museum of Natural History in London or the largest cut star sapphire in existence, the ›Star of India‹ (536 ct) in the American Museum of Natural History in New York, have indeed made history.

The early 20th century saw the onset of a preoccupation with the crystal structure of gemstones in art and architecture. It then became the paramount aesthetic criterion, a new ›law of form‹. The universally acknowledged ›mystique of the precious stone‹ yielded to the ›mystique of the crystal‹. Architects who were exponents of Expressionism dreamed of ›crystalline monuments‹. Futurist painters were inspired by ›crystalline forms‹. They were fascinated by the stringent geometry of these bodies with

Ausschnitt aus: Wenzel Hablik, »Meereszauber«, 1917, Öl auf Leinwand, Wenzel-Hablik-
Stiftung, Itzehoe/D | Detail: Wenzel Hablik, ›The Enchantment of the Sea‹, 1917, oil on
canvas, Wezel-Hablik-Stiftung, Itzehoe/D

träumen von »kristallinen Monumenten«, die Maler des Futurismus lassen sich von
»kristallinen Formen« inspirieren. Sie sind von dem streng geometrischen Körper
mit seinem gesetzmäßigen »Innenbau«, dem sogenannten Kristallgitter, welches die
innere räumliche Struktur widerspiegelt, fasziniert.

So durchzieht der Kristall auch das Werk des Architekten, Malers und Kunstgewerblers
Wenzel Hablik (1881–1934) wie ein roter Faden. Hablik widmet sich in Itzehoe
gleichermaßen der Metallgestaltung wie der Edelsteinschleiferei. Bereits 1908
gelingt es ihm, sich in einer Radiermappe »Schaffende Kräfte« mit der Faszination
des Bergkristalls auseinander zu setzen und sich einen lang gehegten Wunsch zu
erfüllen. In einem Brief des Jahres 1909 an den Kritiker Dr. Ewald Bender erklärt
Hablik seine Radiermappe mit den Worten: »Die Bilder erzählen vom Entstehen und
Werden des Kristalls. In diesem Naturkörper vereinigen sich Reinheit, Klarheit,
Durchsichtigkeit und Schönheit. Vor allem aber lässt sich an ihm ein Grundplan von
Naturgesetzlichkeit ablesen: der Prozess der Kristallisation. Bei eingehendem Studium
erkennt man, wie sich aus einer Grundidee die Vielheit der Erscheinungen entfaltet,
wie ununterbrochenes Werden möglich wird.«[2]

Die indirekte Auseinandersetzung mit dem Kristall spiegelt sich in der revolutionären,
neuen Auffassung einer »kristallinen Welt« aber vor allem in der Architektur wieder.
Auch Wenzel Hablik beschäftigt sich in seinen architektonischen Zeugnissen, mit den
Konsequenzen eines kristallinen Formenrepertoires. Er versetzt Kuben, Hexaeder und
Oktaeder verschiedener Größenordnung in unterschiedlichen Winkeln zueinander,
verschleift die Übergänge durch abermals prismatische Formen und gelangt so zu
neuartigen Turm- und Kuppelgebilden. Hablik will letztendlich das Wort »Bauen«
durch das Wort »Kristallisieren« ersetzen. Die Architekten und Architektur-
schriftsteller Otto Bartning (1883–1959), Walter Gropius (1883–1969) und Bruno
Taut (1880–1938) verwenden ebenfalls das Wort »kristallen« in ihren Aus-
führungen. Kristallformen, sternförmige Grundrisse und mineralische Dekorationen

sind Schlagworte eines »neuen Bauens«. Bereits Bruno Tauts »Glashaus« (Abb. S. 195) für die Werkbundausstellung in Köln 1914 spielt mit dem reflektierenden Licht und seiner Wirkung für den Innenraum. In der Zeitschrift »Frühlicht« von 1920 veröffentlicht Wassily Luckhardt seine »Stadtkrone«, ein Gebäude, das sich ganz klar am Aufbau eines Kristalls orientiert (Abb. S. 195).

Aufbrechende Elemente bestimmen auch die Malerei des Expressionismus, und die Form- und Gestaltungsgesetze der Kubisten und Futuristen sind ebenfalls vom Kristall geprägt. Paul Klee bezeichnet sich 1915 als »Ich, Kristall« und Theodor Däubler nennt den Maler Lyonel Feininger (1871–1956) im Jahre 1919 den »klarsten Kristalliker«.[3] Lyonel Feininger fertigt 1919 zum Bauhausmanifest von Walter Gropius einen Holzschnitt mit dem Titel »die Zukunftskathedrale« (Abb. S. 195); hier steigt die selbst wie ein Kristall aussehende Kathedrale vor einem Hintergrund mit gebrochenen Flächen und strahlenden Sternen auf. Bei Feininger zeigt sich die kristalline Struktur sonst vor allem in seinen kubistischen Straßen- und Architekturbildern, die aus prismatisch gebrochenen, sich überblendenden, kristallinen Formen in transparenten Farbtönen komponiert sind. Aber auch in vielen Holzschnitten

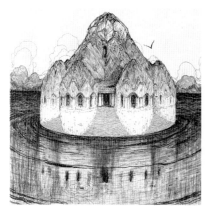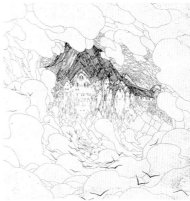

Wenzel Hablik, »Zyklus Schaffende Kräfte«, Blätter 6, 7 und 18, 1909, Radierungen, Wenzel-Hablik-Stiftung, Itzehoe/D ‖ Wenzel Hablik, ›Creative Powers Cycle‹, sheets 6, 7 and 18, 1909, etchings, Wenzel-Hablik-Stiftung, Itzehoe/D

their regular ›inner architecture‹, called the crystal lattice, which mirrors the inner spatial structure.

The crystal runs through the work of Wenzel Hablik (1881–1934), an architect, painter and craftsman, like Ariadne's guiding thread. Hablik devoted himself equally to metalworking and gem-cutting in Itzehoe. As early as 1908 he had managed to satisfy a desire he had long had by investigating the fascination of rock crystal in a portfolio of etchings entitled ›Schaffende Kräfte‹ [›Creative Powers‹]. In a letter written in 1909 to the critic Dr. Ewald Bender, Hablik elucidates his portfolio of etchings as follows: ›The pictures tell of crystal emerging and becoming. Purity, clarity, transparency and beauty are united in this natural body. Above all, however, a ground-plan of the laws of nature can be read in it: the process of crystallisation. By studying this in depth, one realizes how a plurality of phenomena arises from a basic idea, how continual becoming is possible.‹[2]

The study of the crystal is indirectly reflected in the revolutionary new conception of a ›crystalline world‹ and this applies to architecture especially. Wenzel Hablik also studied the consequences of a crystalline repertoire of forms in the architecture that would be his legacy. He arranged cubes, hexahedra and octahedra of varying sizes at varying angles to one another, blurring transitions once again with prismatic forms to achieve innovative tower and dome configurations. What Hablik ultimately strove for was to replace the word ›to build‹ with ›to crystalize‹. Architects and writers on architecture such as Otto Bartning (1883–1959), Walter Gropius (1883–1969) and Bruno Taut (1880–1938) also use the word ›to crystal‹ in their writings. Crystal forms, star-shaped ground-plans and mineral decoration were the buzzwords of a ›new architecture‹. The ›Glass House‹ designed by Bruno Taut for the 1914 Werkbund Exhibition in Cologne plays with reflecting light and its impact on an interior (ill. p. 195). In 1920 the magazine ›Frühlicht‹ published Wassily Luckhardt's ›Stadtkrone‹ [›City Crown‹], a building quite obviously orientated towards the structure of a crystal (ill. p. 195).

Forward-looking elements also shaped expressionist painting and the laws governing the form and configuration of work done by the Cubist and Futurists also derive from the crystal. In 1915 Paul Klee described himself as ›I, crystal‹ and in 1919 Theodor Däubler called the painter

Lyonel Feininger (1871–1956) the ›clearest crystallist‹.[3] In 1919 Lyonel Feininger did a woodcut for Walter Gropius' Bauhaus manifesto entitled ›The Cathedral of the Future‹. Here the cathedral, which looks like a crystal, towers against a background of broken surfaces and radiant stars. Elsewhere in Feininger's work, the structure of crystals appears mainly in Cubist pictures of streets and architecture composed of prismatically broken, irradiating crystalline forms in transparent colour tones. However, crystalline-looking forms also play a major role in numerous woodcuts by other Expressionist artists. In a 1925 Karl Schmidt-Rottluff (1884–1976) woodcut, ›Bergstraße mit großen Kehren und Brücke‹ [›Mountain Road with Turns and Bridge‹], a solid massif seems to have been dissolved into individual crystals.

Like the Expressionist painters and architects who tried to track down the deeper meaning of the crystal, Bernd Munsteiner began to ›look into‹ the crystal as a gem-cutter and to explore its secrets in the 1960s. He was not after the perfect cut or absolute purity in a crystal. What interested him was the crystal in its ›original state‹ rather than the perfectly worked surface and faceting, which

had become a universal plague. He started out by using his knowledge to deal with the original stone, immersing himself in its world – something absolutely new in gem-working.

Thus the artist has succeeded in finding an entirely new approach to stone and working it. He places his creativity and his work at the service of the crystal, directing all his attention to exploring ›hidden treasures‹. Such ›hidden treasures‹ may be mineral inclusions or irregularities in the structure of a crystal. They may be structural changes as well as cavities once filled with liquids or gases. Ultimately they are modifications to the crystal inaugurated by nature itself. Munsteiner is concerned with tracing these irregularities by penetrating the material with all due moderation and respect. In ›reversing‹ the generally accepted valuation of a crystal and viewing its attractions instead in its natural oddities – that is, in its ›impurities‹ – he has opened up uncharted territory which has afforded unsuspected freedoms.

Whereas Hablik was awed by the ›inner beauty‹ of the clear structure of a crystal, Munsteiner is concerned with the ›inner beauty‹ of the ›impurities‹ or the ›pictures‹

Franz Marc, »Der Tiger«, 1912, Öl auf Leinwand, Lenbachhaus München ‖ Franz Marc, ›The Tiger‹, 1912, oil on canvas, Lenbachhaus, Munich

anderer expressionistischer Künstler spielen die kristallin anmutenden Formen eine große Rolle. In dem Holzschnitt »Bergstraße mit großen Kehren und Brücke« von Karl Schmidt-Rottluff (1884–1976) aus dem Jahre 1925 etwa löst sich das massive Gebirge gleichsam in einzelne Kristalle auf.

Ähnlich wie die Maler und Architekten des Expressionismus versuchen, der tieferen Bedeutung des Kristalls nachzugehen, beginnt Bernd Munsteiner in den 1960er Jahren als Edelsteinschleifer in den Kristall »hineinzublicken« und seine eigentliche Struktur mit all ihren Geheimnissen zu erforschen. Er kümmert sich nicht um den perfekten Schliff oder die absolute Reinheit des Kristalls. Ihn interessiert der Kristall im »Urzustand«, nicht die perfekte Oberflächenbearbeitung, die hinlänglich bekannte Facettierung. Er setzt mit seinen Kenntnissen am Urgestein an, taucht in dessen Welt ein – ein absolutes Novum in der Edelsteinbearbeitung.

Dem Künstler gelingt es so, einen ganz neuen Zugang zum Stein und seiner Bearbeitung zu finden. Er stellt sein Schaffen und Wirken in den Dienst des Kristalls. Dem Erforschen der »verborgenen Schätze«, schenkt er seine ganze Aufmerksamkeit. Bei diesen »verborgenen Schätzen« handelt es sich um eingeschlossene Mineralien oder Störungen der Kristallstruktur. Es sind Strukturveränderungen, aber auch Hohlräume, die mit Flüssigkeiten oder Gasen gefüllt waren, letztendlich sind es von der Natur selbst in Gang gesetzte Veränderungen im Kristall. Diesen nachzuspüren, mit gebotenem Maß und Respekt in die Materie einzudringen – das ist Munsteiners Anliegen. Indem der Künstler die allgemein gültige Wertigkeit »verkehrt« und gerade in diesen natürlichen Eigenarten eines Kristalls – also in seinen »Verunreinigungen« – seinen Reiz sieht, öffnet sich ihm ein neues Terrain mit ungeahnten Freiheiten.

War Hablik von der »inneren Schönheit« der klaren Struktur des Kristalls beeindruckt, so ist es bei Munsteiner also die »innere Schönheit« der »Verunreinigungen« oder der »Bilder«, die sich ihm beim Studieren des Steins erschließen und ihn schließlich veranlassen, als Künstler Hand anzulegen.

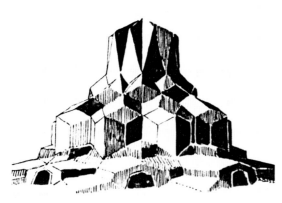  

links: Wassily Luckhardt, »Stadtkrone«, 1920 || **left:** Wassily Luckhardt, ›City Crown‹, 1920 || **Mitte:** Lyonel Feininger, »Die Zukunftskathedrale«, Holzschnitt, 1919 || **centre:** Lyonel Feininger, ›The Cathedral of the Future‹, woodcut, 1919 || **rechts:** Bruno Taut, Glashaus auf der Deutschen Werkbund-Ausstellung, Köln, 1914 || **right:** Bruno Taut, Glass House at the Deutscher Werkbund Exhibition, Cologne, 1914

that open up for him when he is studying a stone and they are what finally inspire him to put his hand to a stone as an artist. Working gemstones and gem-cutting look back on a long tradition in Idar-Oberstein. The minerals mined for centuries in the Hunsrück have made the people living there engage in stone-cutting. And even today the Idar-Obersteiners are past masters at lending gemstones brilliance: the skills of the Idar-Oberstein gem-cutters are highly prized throughout the world.

Bernd Munsteiner, too, learned the classical craft of gem-cutting, which had been practised in his family for two generations before him. Soon after taking his journeyman's certificate, he began training as a jewellery designer at what was then the Werkkunstschule and is now the Fachhochschule für Gestaltung in Pforzheim. Through his studies there, Munsteiner first emancipated himself from the craft he had learned and turned to an intensive preoccupation with designing jewellery. Between 1962 and 1966 he encountered an environment that was extremely constructive: at that time a profound discussion of what jewellery meant as a craft

was sparked off in Pforzheim, as in other centres of jewellery design – including Munich, Hanau, Schwäbisch Gmünd and Düsseldorf – tantamount to a revolution in jewellery design.

A generation of jewellery artists became active who were no longer satisfied with the material value and the artificial beauty of a piece of jewellery – design concepts were now the order of the day, with jewellery coming to express the personal identity of its makers and the wearers alike. At Pforzheim Munsteiner had an opportunity to exchange ideas with people on the same wavelength. He met Robert Smit, Michael Zobel, Wilhelm Buchert, Claus Bury and Günter Krauss, all of them artists who have today gone in different directions. Smit has turned to the avant-garde in Amsterdam and Zobel has found his niche as an innovative jewellery designer at Konstanz on Lake Constance. Bury teaches sculpture. These ›jewellery-makers‹ – as they call themselves – are orientated towards the expressive devices deployed in the visual arts, such as Informel, Tachisme, Op, Pop and Minimal art. Bernd Munsteiner, too, became involved in the art trends of

Bernd Munsteiner zeichnet die Schnitte an einem Stein ein, 2000 ‖ Bernd Munsteiner
drawing the cuts on a stone, 2000

Die Bearbeitung des Edelsteins, die Edelsteinschleiferei, hat in Idar-Oberstein eine
lange Tradition. Die über viele Jahrhunderte im Hunsrück abgebauten Mineralien
veranlassten die dort lebenden Menschen, sich mit dem Schleifen von Steinen zu
beschäftigen. Und man versteht es hier auch heute noch meisterlich, dem Edelstein
seine Brillanz zu verleihen: In weiten Teilen der Welt wird das Können der Edelsteinschleifer von Idar-Oberstein sehr geschätzt.

Auch Bernd Munsteiner erlernt zunächst das klassische Handwerk des Edelstein-
schleifens, das in seiner Familie bereits über zwei Generationen gepflegt wird.
Bald nach der Gesellenprüfung folgt eine weitere Ausbildung zum Schmuckgestalter
an der damaligen Werkkunstschule in Pforzheim, der heutigen Fachhochschule für
Gestaltung. Munsteiner löst sich durch dieses Studium zunächst völlig von seinem
erlernten Handwerk und setzt sich intensiv mit dem Thema Schmuckgestaltung
auseinander. Er trifft zwischen 1962 und 1966 auf ein äußerst glückliches Umfeld:
In Pforzheim, wie auch an anderen Ausbildungsstätten der Schmuckgestaltung –
so etwa in München, Hanau, Schwäbisch Gmünd oder Düsseldorf – setzt zu dieser Zeit
eine tiefgreifende Auseinandersetzung mit dem Schmuckhandwerk ein – eine
Revolution in der Schmuckgestaltung nimmt ihren Anfang.

Es wird eine Generation von Schmuckgestaltern aktiv, denen Materialwert und
künstliche Schönheit eines Schmuckstücks nicht mehr genügt – gestalterische
Konzepte sind gefragt, Schmuck wird zum Ausdruck der eigenen Identität. In
Pforzheim hat Munsteiner Gelegenheit, sich mit Gleichgesinnten auszutauschen, er
lernt unter anderem Robert Smit, Michael Zobel, Wilhelm Buchert, Claus Bury und
Günter Krauss kennen, Künstler, die heute ganz unterschiedliche Wege gehen:
Während sich Smit in Amsterdam der Avantgarde zuwendet und Zobel heute seinen
Platz als innovativer Schmuckgestalter in Konstanz am Bodensee gefunden hat,
arbeitet und lehrt Bury als Bildhauer. Die »Schmuckmacher« – wie sie sich selbst
nennen – orientieren sich an den Ausdrucksmitteln der bildenden Kunst wie dem

Informel, dem Tachismus, der Op-, Pop- und Minimal Art. Auch Bernd Munsteiner setzt sich mit den Kunstströmungen dieser Jahre auseinander. Während seiner Studienjahre trifft er mit dem niederländischen Künstler Jan Schoonhoven (1914–1994) zusammen. Dieser hatte stilistisch zunächst im Umfeld des Surrealismus gearbeitet, in den 1950er Jahren experimentierte er dann mit den Möglichkeiten der informellen Kunst. Schließlich setzte er sich mit der Gruppe »Zero« auseinander, was ihn zu streng seriellen Zeichnungen mit gereihten Linienelementen oder Punktrastern inspirierte. Gerade in dieser Gruppe vollzogen sich damals künstlerische Auseinandersetzungen, die – wenn auch in anderem Material – im Werk Munsteiners ihren Niederschlag fanden. Auf der Grundlage des »Manifesto Blanco« (1946) von Lucio Fontana (1899–1968) war »Zero« 1958 von Heinz Mack (*1931) und Otto Piene (*1923) in Düsseldorf gegründet worden. Beide gehörten zu den Vertretern der kinetischen Kunst, im Werk Heinz Macks zeichnete sich die Auseinandersetzung mit der Op-Art ab, bei Piene lag der zweite Schwerpunkt auf der Lichtkunst. Später schloss sich ihnen Günther Uecker (*1930) an, auch er ein Vertreter der kinetischen Kunst – weitaus bekannter

links: Michael Zobel, Brosche, 1970, Silber, Gold, Bergkristalle (von Bernd Munsteiner) || left: Michael Zobel, brooch, 1970, silver, gold, rock crystals (by Bernd Munsteiner) || **rechts:** Heinz Mack, Lichtrelief, 1959, Aluminium auf Pressspanplatte || right: Heinz Mack, Light Relief, 1959, aluminium on hardboard

those years. While still a student, he met the Dutch artist Jan Schoonhoven (1914–1994). Schoonhoven had started off with stylistic leanings towards Surrealism but by the 1950s he was experimenting with the potential of Informel. He ultimately engaged in discourse with the ›Zero‹ group, which inspired him to create stringently serial drawings with arrayed linear elements or rastering. It was in this group that artistic discourse was engaged in which – albeit in a different material – would precipitate in Munsteiner's work. Founded by Heinz Mack (*1931) and Otto Piene (*1923) in Düsseldorf in 1958, ›Zero‹ was based on Lucio Fontana's (1899–1968) ›Manifesto Blanco‹ (1946). Mack and Piene were exponents of Kinetic art. Heinz Mack's work reveals his exploration of Op art whereas Piene concentrated on Light art. They were later joined by Günther Uecker (*1930), another exponent of Kinetic art – although he is far better known for his ›Nail Pictures‹. All these artists were primarily concerned with light, movement and space. They developed a style which called for the quality of light, motion and material structures as factors in design. The ›quality of light‹ in a gemstone would also become an important design ele-

ment for Bernd Munsteiner, one which can be read in all his works.

Even though the works of Mack, Piene and Uecker are entirely different in articulation, they do have such basic points in common as a tendency to purism, the use of normed, serial basic elements and design according to intelligible, understandable rules within clearly demarcated bounds. Traces of these elements can also be found in the œuvre of the gem sculptor Munsteiner: all cuts he has developed over the years represent deliberate intervention in the stone, which does not allow for too much or too little.

Apart from the artistic influences touched on above, it was his teachers at the Werkkunstschule in Pforzheim who would exert a lasting influence on Bernd Munsteiner's creative work. In the 1960s Klaus Ullrich (1927–1998) and Reinhold Reiling (1922–1983) were actively committed to personally experiencing the then prevailing trends in art. Their preoccupation with the ›guided coincidence‹ provided by Tachisme gave them the scope for a spontaneous approach to designing which is also expressed in a search for new ways of configuring surfaces in jewellery. Fusing on gold, a process seemingly de-structive of that precious metal, also made it possible to reflect on its natural state. Klaus Ullrich, for one, is attracted by richly differentiated, dynamically lively structure rather than artificially polished, ›unnatural‹ surfaces in a piece of jewellery.

Against this background, a ›new spirit‹ was disseminat-ed, revealed not only in the way precious metals were handled and worked. Students, too, felt the urge to seek new possibilities for working gemstones. Professor Karl Schollmayer embarked on building up a field of his own, teaching ›gem design‹ in Pforzheim, since it was appar-ent that new forms and conceptions in jewellery design called for new cuts. Schollmayer summoned Erich Frey to Pforzheim. Frey had trained in Düsseldorf but had also studied the jewellery of indigenous peoples in South Africa, integrating in his own work this distinctively autonomous approach to handling gold and precious stones. The combination of Frey's experiences as an artist and Munsteiner's own consummate skills in gem-cutting led to new approaches to jewellery design in Pforzheim. ›His creativity begins, like any real skill, in

understanding,‹ Schollmayer would later remark on Bernd Munsteiner.

Once back in the Hunsrück, Munsteiner at first devoted himself to the material traditional to the region: agates, with their sophisticated ›inner workings‹. He coaxed new enchantment from them. What he was after was finding new ways for configuring agate reliefs. Where it is found determines the colour scheme of this form of mineral quartz, which is often strongly veined. It can range from brown, red, greyish blue to black.

The workshop run by his grandfather and his father con-centrated primarily on agates since banded agates have always been relatively easy to translate into figurative scenes. Gem-carvers also found the natural properties of the stone very accommodating, as is shown by the many portrait medallions extant. Munsteiner was, therefore, familiar from his earliest years with chalcedony as a ver-satile material that would accompany him on his career for many years. Up to 1995 he frequently returned to working with agates. It is basic to Munsteiner that a par-ticular period of creativity is never really finished. Any theme can be taken up again and retranslated.

allerdings durch seine »Nagelbilder«. Die Beschäftigung mit dem Licht, der Bewegung und dem Raum waren wichtige Anliegen dieser Künstler. Sie entwickelten einen Stil, der die Qualität des Lichts, der Bewegung und materieller Strukturen als Gestaltungsfaktoren propagierte. Die »Qualität des Lichts« im Edelstein wird für Bernd Munsteiner ebenfalls ein wichtiges Gestaltungselement, das sich in allen seinen Werken ablesen lässt.

Wenn sich die Werke von Mack, Piene und Uecker auch völlig unterschiedlich artikulieren, bleiben grundsätzliche Gemeinsamkeiten wie die Neigung zum Purismus, die Verwendung genormter, serieller Grundelemente und die Gestaltung nach einsichtigen, überschaubaren Gesetzen innerhalb klar gesteckter Grenzen. Auch diese Elemente lassen sich im Œuvre des Edelsteinbildhauers Munsteiner ansatzweise nachvollziehen: In allen, über die Jahre entwickelten Schliffformen, zeigt sich das bewusste Setzen von Eingriffen in den Stein, das kein Zuviel oder Zuwenig erlaubt. Neben diesen künstlerischen Einflüssen sind es aber vor allem die Lehrkräfte der Werkkunstschule in Pforzheim, die eine nachhaltige Wirkung auf das künstlerische Schaffen Bernd Munsteiners ausüben. Klaus Ullrich (1927–1998) wie auch Reinhold Reiling (1922–1983) sind in den 1960er Jahren dabei, ihre ganz persönlichen Erfahrungen mit den Kunstströmungen dieser Tage zu machen. Die Auseinander-setzung mit dem »gesteuerten Zufall«, wie ihn der Tachismus bietet, erlaubt ihnen eine spontane Gestaltungsweise, die auch in der Suche nach neuen Wegen für die Oberflächengestaltung im Schmuck zum Ausdruck kommt. Das Anschmelzen des Goldes, ein scheinbar zerstörerischer Vorgang des edlen Metalls, erlaubt gleichzeitig eine Rückbesinnung auf dessen natürlichen Zustand. Klaus Ullrich etwa reizt nicht die künstlich polierte, »unnatürliche« Oberfläche des Schmuckstücks, sondern eine reich differenzierte, dynamisch bewegte Struktur.

Vor diesem Hintergrund breitet sich nicht nur im Umgang und der Bearbeitung edler Metalle ein »neuer Geist« aus, die Studierenden drängt es auch nach neuen Möglichkeiten der Edelsteinbearbeitung. Professor Karl Schollmayer macht sich daran,

CHRISTIANNE WEBER-STÖBER

einen eigenen Lehrbereich für »Edelsteingestaltung« in Pforzheim aufzubauen, denn man erkennt, dass neue Formen und Auffassungen in der Schmuckgestaltung zwangsläufig auch neue Schliffformen für den Edelstein fordern. Schollmayer holt Erich Frey nach Pforzheim. Der in Düsseldorf ausgebildete Künstler hatte sich in Südafrika mit dem Schmuck der Naturvölker auseinandergesetzt und diesen ganz eigenen Umgang mit Gold und edlen Steinen in sein Schmuckschaffen integriert. Mit den künstlerischen Erfahrungen Freys und dem handwerklichen Können des Edelsteinschleifers Munsteiner findet man in Pforzheim zu neuen Wegen in der Schmuckgestaltung. »Seine Kreativität beginnt, wie jedes wirkliche Können, im Erkennen«, bemerkt Schollmayer später über Bernd Munsteiner.

Zurückgekehrt in den Hunsrück, widmet sich Munsteiner zunächst dem traditionellen Material der Region, dem Achat mit seinem vielseitigen »Eigenleben«, und er entlockt ihm neuen Zauber. Sein Augenmerk gilt neuen Wegen der Gestaltung von Achatreliefs. Grundsätzlich bestimmt der Fundort dieses oft mit starken Maserungen durchzogenen Quarzes die Farbgebung, die von Braun, Rot, Graublau bis hin zu Schwarz reicht. Bereits in der Werkstatt des Großvaters und des Vaters werden in erster Linie Achate verarbeitet, denn der Lagenachat erlaubt seit jeher eine relativ einfache Umsetzung figürlicher Szenen. Auch in den vielen Porträtmedaillons kommt die natürliche Beschaffenheit des Steins dem Schleifer sehr entgegen. Munsteiner ist also von Kindesbeinen an mit dem vielschichtigen Chalcedon vertraut, der ihn über viele Jahre seines künstlerischen Schaffens hinweg begleitet. Bis 1995 greift er immer wieder die Arbeit mit dem Achat auf. Grundsätzlich gilt für Munsteiner, dass eine Schaffensperiode niemals endgültig abgeschlossen ist. Jedes Thema kann immer wieder aufgegriffen und neu umgesetzt werden.

»Zu Beginn« so Munsteiner selbst, »versuchte ich graphische, zweidimensionale Elemente in den Achat hineinzuschleifen – vorwiegend auf Onyx oder Carneol.« Im Laufe der Jahre tritt dann die künstlerische Freiheit, die Abstraktion, immer mehr in

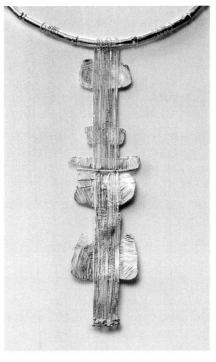

Klaus Ullrich, Halsschmuck, 1966, Gold, Schmuckmuseum Pforzheim/D ||
Klaus Ullrich, neck jewellery, 1966, gold, Schmuckmuseum Pforzheim/D

›In the beginning,‹ says Munsteiner himself, ›I tried to carve graphic, two-dimensional elements into agates – mainly on onyx or cornelian.‹ With time this approach would yield to artistic freedom and abstraction. Ideas were first jotted down in drawings, from which the artist gradually detached himself before the process of translating them into stone could begin.

In the mid-1960s Munsteiner went on a study trip to Jablonek in what was then Czechoslovakia, where he visited the ›Universal Exhibition for Costume Jewellery and Glass Design‹. There he was fascinated to find craftsmanship in glass design built on venerable traditions. He was particularly impressed by the technique of working glass by sandblasting. On his return home, Munsteiner began to blast his agates with corundum grit, which gave new scope for design potential. Wall objects were made in which the relief was enhanced by linear and colour accents underscoring both the structure and the composition of the stone. The reliefs Munsteiner did at that time consist in multiple-layered agates. Blasting them with corundum grit allowed him to penetrate by stages into the material.

In the 1970s his agates, which recall landscapes and organic forms, were still for the most part made from a single piece. By the early 1980s, however, the actual landscape – the typical agate motif – was only suggested in his ›Landscape Scenes‹. The artist has left it up to viewers to open up pictures of their own by using their imagination. In ›Gruppierungen am Abgrund‹ [›Groupings on the Brink of the Abyss‹] (1983) and ›Familien‹ [›Families‹] (1984), the figurative aspect is unmistakable yet actual figures defy detection. Here Munsteiner has gone far beyond his previous approach to design and the traditional formal idiom in agate relief.

Munsteiner was, however, soon thirsting for experiments in a different material enlivened by more light, translucency and depth: he turned to an intensive preoccupation with crystal. Coaxing ›eternally valid beauty‹ from it would become his life's work.

Those little minerals, offered to laymen, collectors and aficionados in innumerable variations and sizes betray virtually nothing of the actual size of the original stone. In the closing lines of Goethe's *Prophesies of Bakis* it says:

Bernd Munsteiner, Brosche, Naturachatrelief, 1977, Gold, 3 Brillanten (siehe auch S. 57) ||
Bernd Munsteiner, brooch, natural agate relief, 1977, gold, 3 diamonds (see also p. 57)

den Vordergrund. Erste Ideen werden in Zeichnungen festgehalten, von denen sich der Künstler allmählich löst bis dann die eigentliche Umsetzung in den Stein beginnt. Mitte der 1960er Jahre unternimmt Munsteiner eine Studienreise nach Jablonek in der damaligen Tschechoslowakei und besucht die »Weltausstellung für Modeschmuck und Glasgestaltung«. Ihn fasziniert das dort auf alte Traditionen aufbauende Handwerk der Glasgestaltung. Insbesondere die technische Bearbeitung des Glases mit dem Sandstrahlgebläse überzeugt ihn. Nach Hause zurück gekehrt, bearbeitet Munsteiner seine Achate jetzt mit einem Korundstrahlgebläse, was ihm neue gestalterische Möglichkeiten bietet. Es entstehen Wandobjekte, bei denen das Relief einen linearen und farblichen Akzent betont, der die Struktur und Komposition des Steins unterstreicht. Munsteiners Reliefs dieser Zeit bestehen aus mehrschichtigen Achaten; das Korundstrahlgebläse erlaubt ihm ein stufenförmiges Eindringen in die Materie.

CHRISTIANNE WEBER-STÖBER

In den 1970er Jahren bestehen die Achate, die an Landschaften und organische Formen erinnern, noch weitgehend aus einem Stück. Bei seinen »Landschaftsszenen« der frühen 1980er Jahre ist die eigentliche Landschaft – das typische Motiv des Achats – nur angedeutet. Der Künstler lässt dem Betrachter die Freiheit, sich mit seiner Phantasie ganz eigene Bilder zu erschließen. In den Arbeiten »Gruppierungen am Abgrund« (1983) und »Familien« (1984) ist das Figurative nicht zu übersehen, ohne dass wirkliche Figuren zu erkennen sind. Munsteiner geht hier weit über den bisherigen Gestaltungsansatz und die traditionelle Formensprache im Achatrelief hinaus.

Bald drängt es Munsteiner aber nach Experimenten in einem anderen Material, in dem mehr Licht, Durchsichtigkeit und Tiefenwirkung lebt: Er wendet sich intensiv dem Kristall zu. Ihm »ewig gültige Schönheit« zu entlocken, wird Munsteiners Lebensaufgabe.

Die dem Laien, Sammler und Liebhaber in unzähligen Variationen und Größen angebotenen kleinen Mineralien, lassen kaum etwas von der eigentlichen Größe des ursprünglichen Steins ahnen. In den letzten Zeilen von Goethes *Weissagungen des Bakis* heißt es:

»Ewig wird er euch sein der Eine, der sich in Viele
Teilt, und Einer jedoch, ewig der Einzige bleibt.
Findet in Einem die Vielen, empfindet die Vielen wie Einen;
Und ihr habt den Beginn, habet das Ende der Kunst.«[4]

Eine Aussage, wie sie den Kristall nicht treffender charakterisieren könnte.

Zum Schleifen und Polieren braucht es größte Sorgfalt und ausgezeichnete Kenntnisse der physikalischen und optischen Eigenschaften der Edelsteine. Struktur, Wesen, Eigenart und Wachstumsverhältnisse der Steine müssen genau erforscht werden. Erst dann lässt sich der gewagte Schritt, das Zersägen eines großen Kristalls, in Angriff nehmen. Oft sind es nicht nur die theoretischen Kenntnisse, die der Stein

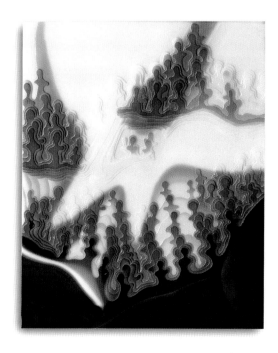

Bernd Munsteiner, Bild »Familien«, 1984, Sarderonyxrelief (siehe auch S. 79) ‖
Bernd Munsteiner, picture ›Families‹, 1984, sardonyx relief (see also p. 79)

Bernd Munsteiner bei der Arbeit an dem Bergkristall »Metamorphose«, 1990 || Bernd
Munsteiner working on the rock crystal ›Metamorphosis‹, 1990

CHRISTIANNE WEBER-STÖBER

dem Künstler abverlangt, es ist das untrügliche Gespür, genau an der richtigen Stelle
anzusetzen. Jedes Mineral besitzt ganz spezielle Eigenschaften, kein Stein gleicht dem
anderen. Munsteiner liebt den Aquamarin, den Turmalin und den Amethyst ebenso
wie den Citrin oder den Bergkristall. Seit 1974 reist der Künstler fast regelmäßig einmal
im Jahr nach Brasilien, um vor Ort auf »Schatzsuche« zu gehen. Im Laufe der Jahre ist
es immer schwieriger geworden, ausgefallene Steine zu finden. Wurden vor einigen
Jahrzehnten noch die in Idar-Oberstein geschliffenen Steine in alle Welt exportiert,
werden die Mineralien inzwischen häufig direkt am Fundort weiter bearbeitet.
Die innere Schönheit eines Kristalls ist schwer zu beurteilen, wenn die zunächst
unförmigen, verkrusteten, grauen bis braunschwarzen Brocken vor einem liegen. Erst
wenn der erste Sägeschnitt vollzogen ist, wird dem Künstler der Blick ins Innere des
Kristalls möglich, öffnet sich ihm eine Welt der ungeahnten Möglichkeiten. Mit seinen
theoretischen Kenntnissen und seiner Erfahrung ist es Bernd Munsteiner möglich, sich
ganz auf die Gestaltung zu konzentrieren.
Zu den Geheimnissen des Kristalls gehört auch seine Farbe. Sie wird durch das Licht,
die Zusammensetzung des Minerals und seine chemischen Spurenelemente
bestimmt. Durch die Lichtbrechung werden gewisse Lichtanteile im Stein vernichtet,
andere erhalten und vom Auge als Farbe wahrgenommen. Bei verschiedenfarbigen
Kristallen kann die plastische Bearbeitung – durch optische Trennung der Farben –
als wichtiges Gestaltungselement eingesetzt werden. »Der Edelsteinschliff erfordert
eine besondere Form von Kreativität. Das Erkennen von Naturformen, den kristallo-
grafischen Aufbau, alles was vorhanden ist, wahrzunehmen, sinnlich zu erfassen.
Das Unsichtbare sichtbar werden zu lassen und einzuordnen. Darauf basiert die
Verwirklichung einer Idee im Mineral, die eigene geistige Aussage«, kommentiert der
Künstler sein Schaffen.
Munsteiner will das Mineral erhalten. Er liebt das Spiel mit der Natur, sie bis an ihre
Grenzen auszureizen ohne sie zu zerstören. Nach wie vor hat für Munsteiner ein
alter Satz aus der Gestaltungslehre Bedeutung, »den Zufall erkennen und die Willkür

ausschließen«. Für ihn gilt, den Stein mit allen seinen »inneren Störungen« zu akzeptieren und gerade darin seine Schönheit zu erkennen. Ein mutiger Schritt, der ihm anfangs auch kritische Stimmen einbringt. Der Erfolg bestätigt ihn bald in seiner Entscheidung: Es gibt immer mehr Verehrer »seiner« Edelsteinkunst.

Im Vordergrund des Gestaltens steht immer der Stein, er hat absolute Priorität, dies gilt auch für die Steine, die in Ketten, Anhängern, Ringen oder Ansteckschmuck Verwendung finden. Als Schmuckgestalter weiß Munsteiner natürlich um die Möglichkeiten im Umgang mit Gold oder Platin als Fassungen und Ergänzungen seiner Stein-Skulpturen. Grundsätzlich wird das Edelmetall dem Stein aber untergeordnet.

Detail aus: Kristall »Dom Pedro«, 1993, Aquamarin (siehe auch S. 128) || Detail: crystal ›Dom Pedro‹, 1993, aquamarine (see also p. 128)

›Eternally will he be to you the one who himself into many Divides and one however who eternally remains the sole.
Find in one the many, feel the many as one;
And you have the be-all and the end-all of art.‹[4]

A statement which aptly characterizes a crystal.
Cutting and polishing gemstones requires the greatest of care and thorough knowledge of their physical and optical properties. The structure, essence, distinctive properties and the conditions under which the stones were formed must be precisely studied. Only then can the bold step of sawing a great crystal be undertaken. Often the stone not only taxes the artist's theoretical knowledge. He must also have an unerring sense of where to start. Every mineral possesses distinctive properties. No stone is exactly like any other. Munsteiner loves aquamarine, tourmaline and amethyst as well as citrine and rock crystal. Since 1974 the artist has gone to Brazil almost every year to ›hunt for treasure‹ at the source. Over the years it has become more difficult to find unusual stones. Only a few years ago stones cut in Idar-Oberstein were still being exported throughout the world. Nowadays, however, minerals are often worked at the place where they are found.

It is difficult to gauge the inner beauty of a crystal when an amorphous, encrusted, grey to brownish black lump is lying before one. Not until the first cut of the saw has been ventured can the artist look into the inside of a crystal revealing a world of unsuspected possibilities. Given his theoretical knowledge and his practical experience, Bernd Munsteiner can concentrate entirely on configuring what is before him.

Colour is one of the secrets of a crystal. It is determined by light and the chemical composition of the mineral, including the trace elements it contains. Through refraction, some parts of the light entering the stone are absorbed by it but others remain and are perceived by the viewer's eye as colour. With pleochroic (showing different colours) crystals, sculptural working — consisting in optically separating the colours — can be used as an important element of design. ›Gem-cutting requires a particular form of creativity. Recognizing natural formations, crystallographic structure, perceiving everything available, grasping all this sensorily. Making visible what is invisible and classifying it. On this is based the realisation of an idea in the mineral, its and one's own intellectual and spiritual statement,‹ is the artist's comment on his approach to his work.

Munsteiner wants to preserve the mineral. He loves playing with nature, testing it to find out its limits, without, however, destroying it. An old principle underlying the dictates of design has retained its validity for Munsteiner: ›Recognize coincidence and rule out arbitrariness‹. He insists on accepting a stone with all its ›inner disturbances‹ and, in fact, recognizing its beauty in just that. A courageous stance which at first also brought him some criticism. However, success was not long in confirming the rightness of his decision. The band of those who admire ›his‹ gemstone art continues to grow.

The stone is always in the foreground when it comes to design. It has absolute priority and this also holds for the stones used in necklaces, as pendants, rings or pins and brooches of various kinds. As a jewellery designer, Munsteiner naturally knows all about the possibilities for handling gold or platinum as settings for and additions to his stone sculptures. Precious metals, however, are always basically subordinated to the stone in his work. There are numerous examples of ingenious composition: harmoniously enhancing elements, deliberate contrasts or immediate reactions to the formal design of a stone. Munsteiner views a crystal as a body in space, approaching it from all sides and angles and using the spatial structure revealed in the inner workings of the crystal. By the time he was a student in Pforzheim, Munsteiner had discovered in crystals the ›reflections‹ which he exploits in his cutting. Over the years he has developed a philosophy of his own in observing the material. He arrives at ›reflecting perspectives‹ ever more frequently. By deliberately using ›hollow cuts‹ on the back, he creates reflections which rekindle the inner life of a mineral. Optical mirroring opens up an entirely individualised approach to the mineral for the viewer.

The first large-scale sculpture dealing with this theme was done in 1984 from a citrine called ›Patriot‹ weighing 64 kg. Again three years later an aquamarine was worked to add an extraordinary sculpture to the ›Reflecting Perspectives‹ series. The body of the crystal, resting on a silver base, soars into an emphatically static con-

Bernd Munsteiner, »Reflektierende Perspektiven«, 1990, Tansanit ‖ Bernd Munsteiner, ›Reflecting Perspectives‹, 1990, tanzanite

Es finden sich zahlreiche Beispiele geschickter Kompositionen: harmonische Ergänzungen, bewusste Kontrastierungen oder direkte Reaktionen auf die formale Gestaltung des Steins.

Munsteiner erfasst den Kristall als räumlichen Körper, nähert sich ihm von allen Seiten und nutzt die räumliche Struktur, die sich im Innern des Kristalls abzeichnet. Bereits während des Studiums in Pforzheim entdeckt Munsteiner in den Kristallen »Reflektionen«, die er für seinen Schliff zu nutzen weiß. Im Laufe der Jahre entwickelt er seine eigene Philosophie in der Betrachtung der Materie, immer häufiger findet er zu den »Reflektierenden Perspektiven«. Durch das bewusste Einsetzen von rückseitigen »Hohlschliffen« entstehen Reflektionen, die das Innenleben des Minerals zu neuem Leben erwecken. Durch optische Verspiegelungen wird dem Betrachter ein ganz eigener Zugang zu dem Mineral erschlossen.

Die erste große Skulptur zu diesem Thema entsteht aus dem 64 kg schweren Citrin »Patriot« im Jahre 1984. Auch mit einem drei Jahre später bearbeiteten Aquamarin wird eine außergewöhnliche Skulptur in der Reihe der »Reflektierenden Perspektiven«

geschaffen: Der auf einem silbernen Sockel sitzende, aufstrebende Körper wird durch die rhythmischen Einschliffe zu einem betont statischen Gebilde, das durch und durch »gestaltet« ist.

»Reflektierende Perspektiven« entdeckt der Künstler immer wieder in den unterschiedlichsten Steinen, im Amethyst, im Turmalin oder im Aquamarin, und macht sie für den Betrachter sichtbar. Bei einem querovalen Amethyst aus dem Jahre 1989 ist es die räumliche Tiefenwirkung, die im Vordergrund steht: Die »Strahlung« des Schliffs lässt sich kaum bündeln, der Betrachter hat Mühe sich auf einen Punkt zu konzentrieren, da die Reflektionen alles überstrahlen. Bei einem Anhänger aus Amethyst/Citrin spielt der Künstler mit der optischen Trennung der beiden Farben des Kristalls: Der Schliff des hochrechteckigen Citrinanteils betont die Vertikalität, der Amethystanteil des Steins bildet das horizontal orientierte »Fundament«.

Unter dem Motto »Natural Movement« verfolgt Munsteiner ab 1985 die Entdeckung der natürlichen Kristallisation des Steins. Seine Einschlüsse oder Strukturveränderungen werden bewusst in den Schliff mit einbezogen.

Edelsteine und Schmuck können sehr erotische Attribute sein, es macht Bernd Munsteiner Freude, diesen Aspekt der künstlerischen Gestaltung bewusst einzusetzen. Im Altertum und im Mittelalter war die Erotik ein unübersehbarer und wesentlicher Bestandteil der Alltagskultur. Erst im Laufe der Jahrhunderte entwickelte sich mit dem zunehmenden Schamgefühl auch ihre differenzierte Darstellung und Wiedergabe in Kunst, Literatur und Musik. Die Erotik ist eine geistig-seelische Entfaltung der Geschlechtlichkeit, ein Spiel mit den Reizen. Sie ist aber zugleich die elementarste Ausdrucksform menschlicher Kommunikation. In der erotischen Kunst wird das Sinnlich-Körperliche, die sexuelle Komponente der Liebe betont. Sie wird aber zugleich auch als integraler Bestandteil der kosmischen Harmonie gesehen.

Für Bernd Munsteiner ist Erotik ein unübersehbares Phänomen des Schmucks: »Für mich ist Schmuck generell etwas Erotisches. Es ist das Spiel zwischen Mann und Frau, das Lust auf Schmuck macht. Warum sollte man sich sonst schmücken? Schmuck

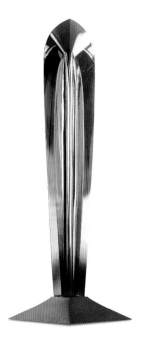

Bernd Munsteiner, Skulptur »Patriot«, 1985, Citrin, Bronze (siehe auch S. 93) ||
Bernd Munsteiner, sculpture ›Patriot‹, 1985, citrine, bronze (see also p. 93)

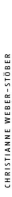

gehört zu dem Spiel, das vor dem eigentlichen Liebesakt zwischen den Geschlechtern stattfindet...«.[5] Bereits 1985/1986 beschäftigt sich Munsteiner mit dem Thema Erotik: »Als ich am Anfang Kerben in Steine geschliffen habe, war das eine Revolution im Edelsteinschleifen. Die Kerbe war für mich ein Gestaltungsmittel«. Diese Einschnitte und Kerben erlauben aber auch die Assoziation zur weiblichen Vagina und bringen das erotische Moment ins Spiel. In der Hamburger Erotik-Ausstellung von 1995 zeigt er Halsschmuck in Gelbgold mit Citrinen und einen Ring mit einem Goldberyll.

Die erotische Komponente findet sich auch in der seit zehn Jahren immer wiederkehrende Beschäftigung Munsteiners mit dem »Symbolon«: Dem Phallussymbol, dem männlichen Attribut wird durch Einschnitte und Kerben das weibliche Element hinzugefügt und es entsteht ein Gleichgewicht zwischen den kosmischen Kräften, wie sie auch im Yin-und-Yang-Prinzip zum Ausdruck kommen.

Angeregt ist das Munteinersche »Symbolon« von der Lingam-Sammlung seines Freundes Günter Krauss in Stuttgart. Das Wort »Lingam« oder auch »Linga« entstammt dem Sanskrit und damit der altindischen Kultur. Es handelt sich um einen Kultstein in Form des männlichen Gliedes, des »Phallus«. Der Lingam-Stein wird in ganz Indien als Symbol für die Gesamtheit der schöpferischen Potenzen Shivas, einem der drei Hauptgötter des Hinduismus verehrt. Es ist ein Flusskiesel, der einen linsenförmigen Einschluss in verschiedenen Farben besitzt. Munsteiner überträgt die formale Gestaltung dieses Steins auf den Kristall.

Das »Symbolon« kann eine kleine Skulptur sein, ein Objekt, im Sinne eines »Handschmeichlers« oder ein Schmuckstück; es taucht als Anhänger oder Kettenglied auf. Immer steht die ausgewogene Vereinigung des männlichen und des weiblichen Elements im Vordergrund: »Die ovale, oblonge, multidimensionale Form des Symbolonschliffes stellt exakt die ihm zugrunde liegende Einheit der Schöpfung dar, für das der Shiva Lingam in den Veden bekannt ist. Nicht zwei konzeptionelle Teile, die zusammengefügt wurden, sondern Ganzheit vom eigentlichen Beginn des kreativen Schaffens [...]« an.[6]

Und doch gibt es auch ein Symbolon–Objekt, das eher das männliche Element in den Vordergrund stellt und das weibliche als künstlerisches Beiwerk zeigt: Der »Fritz-Walter DFB Cup«, der 1994 aus einem Bergkristall mit Rutilnadeln entsteht. Gerade im Symbolon haben die feinen Rutilnadeln, die auch Venushaar oder Liebespfeile genannt werden, eine ganz eigene Bedeutung. Die oblonge Form ist an den Enden mit goldenen Kegeln eingefasst und in einen Kristallsockel eingelassen. Das Symbol des Weiblichen, die Einkerbung, wird hier von einem Goldreif eingefasst, auf dem sich die Inschrift befindet.

Mit jedem neuen, großen Steinfund steht Bernd Munsteiner einer neuen Herausforderung gegenüber, sucht er nach anderen Möglichkeiten der Steinbearbeitung.

Bernd Munsteiner, Fritz Walter DFB Cup »Symbolon«, 1994, Bergkristall mit Rutil (siehe auch S. 135) ‖ Bernd Munsteiner, Fritz Walter DFB Cup ›Symbolon‹, 1994, rock crystal with rutile (see also p. 135)

figuration achieved by rhythmic cuts, a configuration that is thoroughly ›designed‹.

The artist is always discovering ›Reflecting Perspectives‹ in all sorts of stones: in an amethyst, a tourmaline or an aquamarine. Then he makes them visible to viewers. His primary aim with a transversally set ovoid amethyst (1989) was creating spatial depth. The ›rays‹ achieved by the cut can hardly be focused so that viewers have difficulty in concentrating on a single point since the reflections irradiate the whole. The artist plays with dichroism in a pendant of amethyst and citrine. The cut of the upright rectangular citrine part emphasizes the vertical whereas the amethyst part of the stone forms the horizontally aligned ›foundation‹.

With ›Natural Movement‹ as his device, Munsteiner has been following the development of natural crystallisation in stones since 1985. Inclusions or structural modifications are deliberately included in the cut.

Gemstones and jewellery can represent the ultimate in erotic attributes. Bernd Munsteiner delights in making conscious use of this aspect of design. In Greco-Roman antiquity and the Middle Ages, eroticism was an unmis-

takable and quintessential cultural aspect of everyday living. Only over the centuries that followed, with the development of modesty, did it become possible to represent eroticism in the visual arts, literature and music in a sophisticated way. Eroticism is an intellectual and spiritual unfolding of gender as it plays on charm. It is also, however, the elemental form of expression in interpersonal communication. Erotic art emphasizes the sensuous and corporeal, the sexual component of love. Love is also viewed as an integral part of cosmic harmony.

To Bernd Munsteiner, eroticism is a phenomenon so indissolubly linked with jewellery that it cannot be overlooked: ›For me jewellery is generally something erotic. It is the play between man and woman which creates the desire for jewellery. Why should one adorn oneself? Jewellery is part of the foreplay before the actual act of love between the sexes takes place … .‹[5] By 1985/1986 Munsteiner was fully involved with the eroticism theme: ›When I first cut notches into stones, that was a revolution in gem-cutting. The notch was for me a means to configuration.‹ Incisions and notches also permit association with the vagina, bringing the female side of eroticism into play. At the 1995 Hamburg Erotic Exhibition, Munsteiner showed neck jewellery in yellow gold with citrines and a ring set with a golden beryl.

The erotic component has also been there for ten years at least in Munsteiner's recurrent preoccupation with the ›Symbolon‹. The female element is added to the phallus symbol, the male attribute, by means of incisions and notches to create a balance between the cosmic forces as expressed in the Yin and Yang principle.

Munsteiner's rendering of the ›Symbolon‹ has been inspired by the lingam collection owned by a friend in Stuttgart, Günter Krauss. The word ›lingam‹ or ›linga‹ derives from Sanskrit and, therefore, the culture of ancient India. The lingam is a cult stone in the form of the male member, the ›phallus‹. Throughout India, the lingam stone is venerated as symbolizing the creative potency of Shiva, one of the three main gods of the Hindu pantheon. It is riverine alluvial shingle possessing a lentoid inclusion in various colours. Munsteiner transfers the formal design of such stones to crystal.

A ›Symbolon‹ may be a small-scale sculpture, an object that ›nestles in one's palm‹, or a piece of jewellery. It appears as a pendant or as an element of a necklace. The balanced union of the male and female elements is invariably emphasised: ›The oval, oblong, multi-dimensional form of a Symbolon cut represents precisely the unity of creation underlying it, for which the Shiva lingam is known in the Vedas. Not two conceptional parts that have been fitted together but wholeness from the actual onset of creativity [...].‹[6]

Yet there is also a Symbolon object which tends to underscore the male element, with the female element subordinated to parergon status: the ›Fritz Walter DFB Cup‹, made from a rock crystal with enclosed needle-like crystals of rutile in 1994. In the Symbolon especially, the fine, needle-like forms of rutile, also known as ›Venus Hair‹ or in German as ›Cupid's darts‹, have assumed particular significance. The oblong form is set with gold cones at both ends and set into a crystal base. The female symbol, the notch, is here set in a gold bangle with an inscription on it.

Each stone he finds confronts Bernd Munsteiner with a fresh challenge. He has to discover different possibilities for working each one. A rock crystal with needle-like rutile inclusions, found at Bahia, Brazil, and weighing

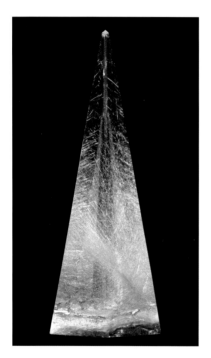

Bernd Munsteiner, Skulptur »Metamorphose«, 1990, Bergkristall mit Rutil, Michael M. Scott Collection (siehe auch S. 109) ‖ Bernd Munsteiner, sculpture ›Metamorphosis‹, 1990, rock crystal with rutile, Michael M. Scott Collection (see also p. 109)

Ein Bergkristall mit Rutilnadeln von 830 Kilogramm, in Bahia in Brasilien gefunden, stellt Bernd Munsteiner im Jahre 1990 vor eine noch nicht gekannte Herausforderung. Als er auf einer seiner Reisen in Brasilien von dem außergewöhnlichen Fund erfährt, steht für ihn fest, dass er sich um diesen Stein »kümmern muss«. Auch wenn man der rauen Oberfläche zunächst nicht ansehen kann, was sich im Innern wirklich verbirgt, beschließt Munsteiner, diesen riesigen Bergkristall in sein Atelier nach Deutschland bringen zu lassen.

Der erste Ansatz, diesen Stein zu zerteilen, erfolgt in einer tagelangen Prozedur. Es gelingt schließlich, den Stein im unteren Drittel in zwei Stücke zu zersägen und zu öffnen. Es bietet sich dem Künstler ein grandioses Schauspiel, das ihm bisher nicht begegnet ist und sich wohl kein zweites Mal wiederholen wird. Nach einem Jahr ist die einzigartige Verwandlung vollzogen und die Plastik erhält den Namen »Metamophose I«: ein 97 kg schwerer Bergkristall mit einem Feuer von Rutilnadeln, die sich zentrifugal, einem Wirbel ähnlich, über den Stein hin ausbreiten.

Der »Metamorphose«, der Gestaltwandlung oder Verwandlung im Allgemeinen begegnen wir in der Botanik und in der Zoologie. Die Entstehung des Minerals selbst ist in gewissem Sinne als eine Art »Metamorphose« zu verstehen. Die erzählende Dichtung der Antike hat uns die »Metamorphosen« des römischen Dichters Ovid überliefert, in denen es um die Verwandlungen von Menschen in Tiere und Pflanzen geht. Bei den kristallinen Metamorphosen Bernd Munsteiners handelt es sich um die künstlerische Umwandlung eines hexagonalen Kristalls in eine frei gestaltete Plastik. Neue, der Materie entsprechende Sehräume werden geschaffen, durch die Reflektion des Lichtes neue illusionistische Bilder erzeugt. Es ist faszinierend, die Entstehungs- geschichte einer solchen »Metamorphose« zu verfolgen, auch wenn sie nur eine ganz vage Vorstellung von dem wirklichen Ausmaß der Arbeit vermitteln kann.

Im selben Jahr beginnt die Arbeit an »Metamorphose II«, und es gelingt dem Künstler auch hier ein Meisterwerk. Wieder setzt Munsteiner seine Einschnitte,

Bernd Munsteiner, »Inside Selecting«, 1992, Amethyst, Michael M. Scott Collection (siehe auch S. 122) || Bernd Munsteiner, ›Inside Selecting‹, 1992, amethyst, Michael M. Scott Collection (see also p. 122)

830 kilograms, presented Bernd Munsteiner with a challenge on an unprecedented scale in 1990. When he heard about the unusual find on one of his trips to Brazil, he realised at once that he had to ›see to‹ that stone. Even though the rough surface of the raw stone revealed at first sight nothing of what is concealed within, Munsteiner decided to have the gigantic rock crystal shipped to his studio in Germany.

The first approach to dividing up this stone was a protracted procedure that took several days. Finally he managed to saw the lower third of the stone into two pieces and to open it. It presented the artist with an awesome spectacle he had never before encountered and probably never will again. It took a year to complete this unprecedented transformation and the ensuing sculpture was given the name ›Metamorphose I‹ [›Metamorphosis I‹]: a rock crystal weighing 97 kg with a blaze of needle-like rutile inclusions spreading out in a centrifugal swirl over the stone.

The ›Metamorphosis‹, a transformation or general change in form, occurs in nature in both flora and fauna and is studied accordingly in botany and zoology. The formation of a mineral represents in itself a sort of ›Metamorphosis‹.

Roman literature has bequeathed to us the ›Metamorphoses‹ of the poet Ovid, which are about the transformation of human beings into animals and plants. Bernd Munsteiner's crystalline metamorphoses concern the artistic transformation of an hexagonal crystal into a free sculpture. New visual spaces matching the material are created and new, illusionist images are generated by the reflection of light. It is fascinating to trace the genesis of a ›Metamorphosis‹ of this kind even though doing so can only convey a vague idea of the actual scale of the work involved.

That year saw work begin on ›Metamorphose II‹ [›Metamorphosis II‹] and again the artist brought forth a masterpiece. Munsteiner again placed his incisions, his notches, across the edge of the stone. They direct and guide the viewer's gaze to an ›explosion‹ of needle-like rutile inclusions, whose centre of gravity is in the lower third of the work.

The years that followed saw more ›Metamorphoses‹, some of them on a smaller scale – each work was a one-off piece, with no two alike. A particularly remarkable sculpture is the 1991 ›Metamorphose VI‹ [›Metamorphosis VI‹]:

Kristall »Dom Pedro«, 1993, Aquamarin (siehe auch S. 128) ‖ Crystal ›Dom Pedro‹, 1993, aquamarine (see also p. 128)

seine Einkerbungen über die Kante des Steins, sie lenken und führen den Blick des Betrachters auf eine »Explosion« von Rutilnadeln, die sich schwerpunktmäßig im unteren Drittel der Arbeit befinden.

In den nachfolgenden Jahren entstehen weitere, auch kleinere »Metamorphosen« – jedes Werk ein unvergleichliches Unikat. Besonders zu erwähnen ist die Skulptur »Metamorphose VI« aus dem Jahre 1991: In dem aufstrebenden Körper, der sich nach oben verjüngt, herrscht ein »Gewitter« von sich überkreuzenden Rutilnadeln. In diese »Unruhe« setzt Munsteiner seinen in der Mitte aufsteigenden Schliff, der sich wie ein Doppelband von kleineren und größeren geometrischen Formen bis in die Spitze hinaufzieht und dem Blick des Betrachters die Richtung weist. Munsteiner arbeitet hier mit dem Kontrast der natürlichen, »diffusen« Verteilung der Rutilnadeln und dem bewussten Eingriff in den Stein.

Eine Stele aus Citrin von 1986 sei hier beispielhaft für die Philosophie des »Inside Selecting« genannt. Das Thema findet sich auch bei einem Halsschmuck mit Citrin aus dem Jahre 1991. Zwei Diamantdreiecke akzentuieren den Stein im Mittelpunkt, Gelbgold und Platin ergänzen den Stein und machen ihn erst zum tragbaren Schmuckstück.

Im Laufe der Jahre werden die »Reflektierenden Perspektiven« und »Inside Selecting« gelegentlich durch rhythmisierende und damit betont strukturierende Einschnitte ergänzt. Bei »Rhythmus V« ist eine Citrin-Halbscheibe an einer Ecke abgekantet und so in ihrer statischen Ruhe gestört. Diese Belebung setzt sich in »seismographischen« Einschnitten fort, die sich scheinbar gleichmäßig in einem schmalen Band über die Fläche hinziehen.

In dem Halsschmuck »Rhythmus« aus dem Jahre 1991, ist ein Beryll der Mittelpunkt. Der Kristall ist vertikal ausgerichtet. Die von oben nach unten verlaufenden Schliffe werden immer kleiner und bilden einen rhythmischen Verlauf. Die Rhythmisierung im Schliff setzt sich auch in den gleichen, sechseckigen goldenen Gliedern der Kette fort.

CHRISTIANNE WEBER-STÖBER

Bereits in einem quadratischen Anhänger aus dem Jahre 1974 wird die strenge Form des in Gold gefassten Citrins durch in der Mitte leicht schräg angesetzte Einschnitte aufgehoben. Die stromlinienförmige Akzentuierung wird durch in Platin ausgeführte Dreiecke, die wie Spitzen aus dem Quadrat herausragen, noch betont.

Grundsätzlich steht für Bernd Munsteiner bei der Bearbeitung seiner Steine die bewusste Wahrnehmung, die intensive Auseinandersetzung mit dem Kristall im Vordergrund – erst dann wagt der Künstler den Schritt, seine Vorstellungen umzusetzen.

Es ist für Bernd Munsteiner immer eine spannende Geschichte, sich einem großen Stein das erste Mal zu nähern, ihn in Augenschein zu nehmen und schließlich Hand anzulegen. In ganz besonderem Maße gilt dies für so außergewöhnliche Steine wie den Aquamarinrohkristall »Dom Pedro« aus Minas Gerais in Brasilien, der – mit einem Rohgewicht von 25 875 Gramm und einer Höhe von 59 cm – seinen Namen nach den beiden Kaisern Dom Pedro I und Dom Pedro II von Brasilien erhielt.

In sechs Monaten wurde aus diesem riesigen Aquamarin-Rohling der Obelisk »Dom Pedro« geschaffen, der selbst noch ganze 35 cm hoch ist und 10 363 ct wiegt. Erst nach genauem Studium der Eigenschaften dieses Steines wie Einschlüsse, Risse, Sprünge und des Farbenspiels konnte sich Munsteiner an den hellblauen

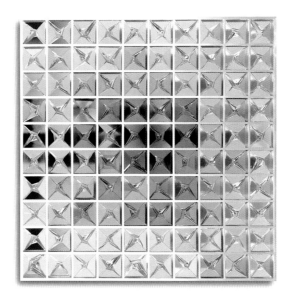

Bernd Munsteiner, Bild »Millennium-Kristall-Reflexionen«, 2000, Bergkristall, Rauchquarz, Citrin, Aluminium, Stahl (siehe auch S. 171) || Bernd Munsteiner, picture ›Millennium Crystal Reflections‹, 2000, rock crystal, smoky quartz, citrine, aluminium, steel (see also p. 171)

a ›thunderstorm‹ of rutile inclusions crossing each other (sagenite, from Latin *sagena*, meaning a ›large fishing net‹) in a soaring body tapering towards the top. Munsteiner has set his cut, which rises at the centre, in this ›turbulence‹ to climb up and around like a double border of small and larger geometric forms spiralling to the tip, thus showing viewers the direction in which to look. Munsteiner is in this case working with the contrast between the natural ›diffuse‹ distribution of the needle-like rutile inclusions and his deliberate intervention in the stone.

A stele of citrine (1986) exemplifies the philosophy of ›Inside Selecting‹. This theme recurs in citrine neck jewellery in 1991. Two diamond triangles emphasize the centre of the stone. Yellow gold and platinum enhance it, turning it into a wearable piece of jewellery.

Over the years ›Reflecting Perspectives‹ and ›Inside Selecting‹ have occasionally been linked with cutting which is rhythmicising and, therefore, emphatically structuring. In ›Rhythmus V‹ [›Rhythm V‹], one tip of a semicircle of citrine has been chamfered, which has disturbed the equilibrium of its statics. This enlivening intervention continues in ›seismographic‹ incisions which seem to extend uniformly across the surface in a narrow band.

A beryl is the centre of attraction of ›Rhythmus‹ (1991), a piece of neck jewellery. The crystal is aligned with its vertical axis. The cuts running from top to bottom dwindle in size to form a rhythmic course. This rhythmicizing cut continues on to the uniform hexagonal gold links of the necklace.

As early as 1974 Munsteiner was subverting the astringent form of a citrine pendant forming a square set in gold by deploying slightly oblique cuts at the centre. The streamlining effect created by this emphasizing touch is further enhanced by triangles executed in platinum which stick out of the square in points.

Fundamental to Bernd Munsteiner's approach to working his stones are perceptive awareness of them and intensive study of the crystals – not until these factors have been satisfactorily addressed does the artist begin to translate his ideas.

It is always exciting for Bernd Munsteiner to approach a large stone for the first time, subject it to close observation and then finally laying a hand on it. This is especially true of unusual stones such as ›Dom Pedro‹, a raw aquamarine crystal from Minas Gerais, Brazil. Weighing 25 875 grammes and measuring 59 cm in height in its raw state, it was named after the first two emperors of Brazil, Dom Pedro I and Dom Pedro II.

It took six months to turn this gigantic raw aquamarine into ›Dom Pedro‹, an obelisk which still measures 35 cm in height and weighs 10 363 ct. Munsteiner did not venture to approach this enormous light blue crystal until he had thoroughly studied such properties of the stone as inclusions, fissures, cracks and the play of colour. The back of the stone has been worked with wavy cutting, an allusion to the close affinity between aquamarine and the sea, which ultimately also gave this sculpture the name of ›Ondas Maritimas‹. ›Dom Pedro‹ is the largest cut aquamarine of gemstone quality in the world. The raw material remaining from it even yielded sculptures on a smaller scale.

In 1997 Bernd Munsteiner handed his studio over to his son Tom so that he could concentrate on his passion for sculpture and objects. Munsteiner's more recent work includes ›Wall Ornaments‹ (ill. p. 211). These are wall pictures composed of individual geometrically cut and arranged rock crystals, citrines, smoky quartz and rutile quartz set into a ›scaffold‹ of light metal. The stones are juxtaposed to create a pictorial texture distinguished by chatoyancy and variations in cut.

›Millenium–Kristall–Reflexionen‹ [›Millennium Crystal Reflections‹] is the largest ›Wall Ornament‹, which is composed of a hundred cut citrines. As an aesthetic whole,

Bernd Munsteiner, Skulptur »Blue Quartz Millennium«, 1999, blauer Quarz (siehe auch S. 183) ‖ Bernd Munsteiner, sculpture ›Blue Quartz Millennium‹, 1999, blue quartz (see also p. 183)

Riesenkristall heranwagen. Die Rückseite des Steins ist mit wellenartigen Einschnitten bearbeitet, die auf die enge Verbundenheit zwischen Aquamarin und Meer hinweisen und schließlich der Skulptur auch den Namen »Ondas Maritimas« gaben. »Dom Pedro« ist der weltweit größte geschliffene Aquamarin in Edelsteinqualität. Aber auch aus dem verbliebenen Rohmaterial wurden noch kleinere Skulpturen geschaffen.

Im Jahre 1997 übergibt Bernd Munsteiner sein Atelier seinem Sohn Tom, um sich mehr seiner Leidenschaft, den Skulpturen und Objekten widmen zu können. Zu den neueren Arbeiten Munsteiners gehören die »Wall Ornaments« (Abb. S. 211). Diese Wandbilder setzen sich aus einzelnen, geometrisch geschliffenen und angeordneten Bergkristallen,

Citrinen, Rauchquarzen und Rutilquarzen zusammen und sind in ein »Gerüst« aus Leicht-
metall eingefügt. Die Steine sind so nebeneinander gesetzt, dass eine Bildstruktur entsteht, die sich durch farbliche Changierungen und unterschiedliche Schliffe auszeichnet.
Das größte »Wall Ornament« ist die Arbeit »Millenium-Kristall-Reflexionen«, ein Bild
aus einhundert geschliffenen Citrinen, das in seiner geschlossenen Flächigkeit dem
Charakter eines Tafelbildes sehr nahe kommt.

Mit dem »Blue Quartz Millenium« schuf Bernd Munsteiner im Jahre 1999 ein weiteres
Werk, das beispielhaft für die Bearbeitung eines sehr großen Quarzes steht. Aus
einem brasilianischen, blau gebänderten, ursprünglich 2000 Kilogramm schweren
Quarz, ist eine 1,51 m hohe Skulptur entstanden – ein Wahrzeichen für den Eintritt
ins 21. Jahrhundert, das auf dem Robert Mouawad Campus des Gemmological
Institute of America in Carlsbad (Kalifornien) steht. Nur dank des großzügigen
Sponsorings von Julius Sauer aus Rio de Janeiro in Brasilien, war es Bernd Munsteiner
möglich, sich an diese große Aufgabe heranzuwagen.

Eigentlich ist der Diamant nicht Bernd Munsteiners bevorzugter Stein, und nur selten
beschäftigt sich der Künstler mit dem Thema Design im Sinne der Entwicklung eines
Entwurfs als Prototyp und dessen formaler Umsetzung in Serie. Dennoch entwickelt

Bernd Munsteiner am Schleifrad, 1993 ‖ Bernd Munsteiner at the cutting wheel, 1993

this picture surface approaches the character of a panel
painting.
›Blue Quartz Millennium‹ (1999) exemplifies yet again
Bernd Munsteiner's approach to working a quartz on a
very large scale. A Brazilian blue-banded quartz that
originally weighed 2000 kilograms was turned into a
sculpture 1.51 m high – a landmark signalizing the entry
into the 21st century set up on the Robert Mouawad
Campus of the Gemmological Institute of America in
Carlsbad, California. Bernd Munsteiner could not have
ventured on this daunting task without the generous
sponsoring of Julius Sauer of Rio de Janeiro, Brazil.
The diamond is really not Bernd Munsteiner's favourite
stone so he rarely works on diamond design in the sense
of developing a prototype and translating it into serial
execution. Still, in 1990, he did develop a new cut,
what he has called the ›Context Diamond‹, for the firm
of Dr. Ulrich Freiesleben, from the basic form of the

natural diamond octahedral crystal structure, exploiting
the maximum capacity of the material to reflect light.
It was high time after so many years, even centuries by
now, to replace the dominance of the brilliant cut with a
contemporary one which would also be appropriate for
modern jewellery design. Bernd Munsteiner has helped
the diamond to innovative form with his new cut. As
always, Munsteiner is exceedingly careful with what
nature has presented him. The prescribed number of
eight surfaces was accepted. The cut advanced to the
point that the maximum reflection of light was attained.
This stunning achievement was awarded a ›Red Point
for Highest Quality in Design‹. Not long afterwards Munsteiner followed it up by going a step further to develop
the ›Spirit Diamond‹. Here, too, the aim is to attain the
maximum concentration of light rays – in this case
achieved by a round diamond cut. The ›Context Cut‹
and ›Spirit Sun‹ cuts have fallen on fertile ground at

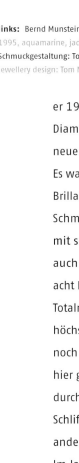

CHRISTIANNE WEBER-STÖBER

links: Bernd Munsteiner, Ring »Context Cut«, 1995, Aquamarin, Jade, Platin (siehe S. 157) ‖ **left:** Bernd Munsteiner, ring ›Context Cut‹, 1995, aquamarine, jade, platinum (see also p. 157) ‖ **rechts:** Bernd Munsteiner, Ring »Spirit Sun«, 1997, Peridot, Achatrelief, Gold; Schmuckgestaltung: Tom Munsteiner (siehe auch S. 158) ‖ **right:** Bernd Munsteiner, Ring ›Spirit Sun‹, 1997, peridot, agate relief, gold; jewellery design: Tom Munsteiner (see also p. 158)

er 1990 für die Firma Dr. Ulrich Freiesleben aus der Grundform des natürlichen Diamantoktaeders unter Berücksichtigung der Totalreflexion des Materials, einen neuen Schliff, den sogenannten »Context Diamond«.

Es war sicher schon längst an der Zeit, den über viele Jahrhunderte allein gültigen Brillantschliff durch einen zeitgemäßen Schliff zu ersetzen, der auch der modernen Schmuckgestaltung entgegen kommt. Bernd Munsteiner verhilft dem Diamanten mit seinem neuen Schliff zu einer innovativen Form. Wie immer geht Munsteiner auch hier sehr behutsam mit der Vorgabe der Natur um. Die vorgegebene Anzahl von acht Flächen wird respektiert und der Schliff soweit vorangebracht, dass sich die Totalreflexion des Lichtes einstellt. Die Auszeichnung mit dem »Roten Punkt« für höchste Designqualität bestätigt diese Leistung. Kurze Zeit später geht Munsteiner noch einen Schritt weiter und entwickelt den sogenannten »Spirit Diamond«. Auch hier geht es wieder um die extrem hohe Bündelung des Lichts – nun aber erzielt durch einen runden Diamantschliff. Die Firma Wild & Petsch hat es verstanden, die Schliffe »Context-Cut« und »Spirit-Sun« auch für Turmalin, Peridot, Aquamarin und andere farbige Edelsteine fruchtbar zu machen.

Im Jahre 1991 fasziniert Bernd Munsteiner außerdem der für ihn ungewöhnliche Auftrag des dänischen Unternehmens Royal Copenhagen, Objekte aus Glas zu entwerfen und herzustellen. Es entsteht eine Serie von etwa 50 zwischen 40 und 50 cm hohen Plastiken. Sie sind in leuchtenden Farben in verschiedenen Rottönen gehalten, die in ihren Schattierungen den Zauber und die Glut des Glases vermitteln. Es handelt sich um kugelartige Objekte oder auch in die Höhe strebende, teilweise geschliffene Arbeiten. Als Unikate besitzen sie jeweils eine ganz eigene Ausstrahlung. Und doch fehlt diesen Glasobjekten das bizarre Innenleben, das Munsteiner bei den Kristallen so fasziniert. Die Glasobjekte und die Diamantschliffe sind für Munsteiner Experimente und bleiben denn auch eine Ausnahme in seinem Werk. Als Ganzes bietet das Œuvre Bernd Munsteiners eine völlig neue Sichtweise auf den Edelstein in seiner jeweiligen Besonderheit – fernab von den traditionellen Vorstellungen seines merkantilen oder symbolischen Wertes. Bernd Munsteiner selbst sieht seine Arbeiten – seine Skulpturen und auch seinen Schmuck – als künstlerische Zeit-Zeugen, die eindeutig von seiner persönlichen Aussage geprägt sind. Wenn er zu Mineralien greift, die oft mehr als zweihundert Millionen Jahre lang tief in der Erde ruhten, dann werden sie unter seiner Hand in einen neuen Zustand, in ein »Zwischenstadium« ihres Seins versetzt, um so unendlich viele Jahre, vielleicht für die Ewigkeit, weiter existieren zu können.

[1] Phil. Schmidt, S. J.: Das Steinbuch des Aristoteles, in: Sonderheft zur Zeitschrift der Deutschen Gesellschaft für Edelsteinkunde. Prof. Dr. Karl Schlossmacher zum 70. Geburtstag, Idar-Oberstein 2, 1957, S. 89.

[2] Wolfgang Reschke, Wenzel Hablik 1881–1934 in Selbstzeugnissen und Beispielen seines Schaffens, Ausst.-Kat., Münsterdorf 1981, S. 84.

[3] Klaus-D. Pohl, Sinnbild Neuen Lebens. Kristall und Kristallisation in der Kunst des 19. und 20. Jahrhunderts, in: Katalog »Faszination Edelstein. Aus den Schatzkammern der Welt. Mythos. Kunst. Wissenschaft«, Ausstellungskatalog Hessisches Landesmuseum Darmstadt, Darmstadt 1992.

[4] Goethes Weissagungen des Bakis entstanden in Weimar zwischen 1798 und 1805, vgl: Heinz Nicolai (Hg.), Goethes Gedichte in zeitlicher Folge, Frankfurt 1982, S. 485.

[5] Günter Krauss (Hg.), Erotischer Schmuck, Ausst.-Kat. Erotic Art Museum Hamburg, Stuttgart 1995, S. 69.

[6] Auszug aus dem Text: Guido Figdor, »Symbolon« – Bernd Munsteiners neues Edelsteindesign inspiriert durch das ewige Wissen des Veda, [Typoskript] 1994.

Bernd Munsteiner, Skulptur, 1991, farbiges Glas, Entwicklung für Royal Copenhagen/DK (siehe auch S. 119) || Bernd Munsteiner, sculpture, 1991, coloured glass, developed for Royal Copenhagen, DK (see also p. 119)

Wild & Petsch, who have used them for tourmalines, peridot, aquamarine and other coloured gemstones. In 1991 Bernd Munsteiner was also enthusiastic about an unusual commission he received from Royal Copenhagen of Denmark to design and make glass objects. A series of about fifty sculptures ranging between 40 and 50 cm in height has come out of it. They glow in reds, their shading conveying the enchantment and fire of the glass. These are spherical objects or vertically orientated works, some of them cut. Each is a one-off with its own distinctive aura. Yet these glass objects lack the bizarre inner life which Munsteiner finds so enthralling in crystals. The glass objects, like the diamond cuts, are experiments as far as Munsteiner is concerned so they remain the exception rather than the rule in his work.

On the whole, Bernd Munsteiner's œuvre conveys an entirely new perspective on gemstones and their respective properties – at a far remove from traditional notions of their market valuation or even their symbolic or intrinsic value. Bernd Munsteiner himself views his work – his sculpture as well as his jewellery – as bearing artistic eyewitness to the times and as unequivocally shaped by the personal statements he is making. When he reaches for minerals which have often lain deep in the earth for more than two million years, his hands put them into a new state, a ›transitional stage‹ of their ontology so that they can thus continue to exist for endless years, perhaps for eternity.

[1] Phil. Schmidt, S. J.: Das Steinbuch des Aristoteles, in: Sonderheft zur Zeitschrift der Deutschen Gesellschaft für Edelsteinkunde. Prof. Dr. Karl Schlossmacher zum 70. Geburtstag, Idar-Oberstein 2, 1957, p. 89.

[2] Wolfgang Reschke, Wenzel Hablik 1881–1934 in Selbstzeugnissen und Beispielen seines Schaffens, exhib. cat., Münsterdorf 1981, p. 84.

[3] Klaus-D. Pohl, Sinnbild Neuen Lebens. Kristall und Kristallisation in der Kunst des 19. und 20. Jahrhunderts, in: ›Faszination Edelstein. Aus den Schatzkammern der Welt. Mythos. Kunst. Wissenschaft‹, exhib. cat. Hessisches Landesmuseum Darmstadt, Darmstadt 1992.

[4] Goethe's Prophesies of Bakis were written in Weimar between 1798 and 1805: cf: Heinz Nicolai (ed.), Goethes Gedichte in zeitlicher Folge, Frankfurt 1982, p. 485.

[5] Günter Krauss (ed.), Erotischer Schmuck, exhib. cat. Erotic Art Museum Hamburg, Stuttgart 1995, p. 69.

[6] Text excerpt: Guido Figdor, ›Symbolon‹ – Bernd Munsteiners neues Edelsteindesign inspiriert durch das ewige Wissen des Veda, [typescript] 1994.

ANHANG

APPENDIX

BIOGRAFIE

1943	geboren am 2. März in Mörschied bei Idar-Oberstein, Deutschland
1957–1960	Ausbildung als Edelsteinschleifer bei seinem Vater Viktor Munsteiner in Idar-Oberstein, dann Gesellenprüfung
1962–1966	Studium an der Fachhochschule für Gestaltung in Pforzheim, Deutschland, bei Prof. Schollmayer und Prof. Ullrich
1966	Staatsexamen als Gestalter für Edelsteine und Schmuck
seit 1966	Freischaffend tätig als Gestalter für Edelsteine und Schmuck
seit 1973	Atelier in Stipshausen bei Idar-Oberstein, Deutschland

Arbeiten in nationalen und internationalen Sammlungen und Museen

MITGLIEDSCHAFTEN

Berufsverband Bildender Künstler Rheinland-Pfalz (BBK)

Gesellschaft Material + Form

The Guild of Contemporary American Jewelry Design

International Jewelry Design Guild Inc.

BIOGRAPHY

1943	born on 2 March in Mörschied near Idar-Oberstein, Germany
1957–1960	Training as a gem-cutter with his father, Viktor Munsteiner, in Idar-Oberstein, followed by apprenticeship examination
1962–1966	Studied at Fachhochschule für Gestaltung in Pforzheim, Germany, with Professors Schollmayer and Ullrich
1966	State examinations in gem and jewellery design
since 1966	Freelance gem and jewellery designer
since 1973	Studio in Stipshausen near Idar-Oberstein, Germany

Works in collections and museums in Germany and worldwide

MEMBERSHIPS

Berufsverband Bildender Künstler Rheinland-Pfalz (BBK)
Gesellschaft Material + Form
The Guild of Contemporary American Jewelry Design
International Jewelry Design Guild Inc.

AUSZEICHNUNGEN (AUSWAHL)

1968	Förderpreis für das Kunsthandwerk Rheinland-Pfalz/D
1969	Goldmedaille, Handwerksmesse München/D
1974	Staatspreis für das Kunsthandwerk Rheinland-Pfalz/D
1980	Auszeichnung, Staatspreis für das Kunsthandwerk Rheinland-Pfalz/D
1981	1. Preis, Künstler-Wettbewerb »Architektur-Kleinplastik«, Mainz/D
1981	Gold- und Bronzemedaille, Zlatarska Razstava Celjy/YUG
1983	Ehrenmitglied, Worshipful Company of Goldsmiths, London/GB
1984	1. und 2. Preis, Deutscher Schmuck- und Edelsteinpreis, Idar-Oberstein/D
1987	1. Preis, Deutscher Schmuck- und Edelsteinpreis, Idar-Oberstein/D
1992	1. Preis, Prix Arctica, Kemi Art Museum, Kemi/FIN
1996	Ehrenmitglied, The American Gem Trade Association, Inc.
1997	Auszeichnung für höchste Designqualität, Design Zentrum Nordrhein-Westfalen/D (für »Context-Cut«)
1999	Contemporary Design Group Award, Hall of Fame, Las Vegas/USA
2001	Anerkennung für Produktdesign, Designpreis Rheinland-Pfalz/D

AWARDS (A SELECTION)

1968	Förderpreis für das Kunsthandwerk Rhineland-Palatinate/D	1996	Honorary Life Member, The American Gem Trade Association, Inc.
1969	Gold medal, Handwerksmesse Munich/D	1997	Distinction for Top Design Quality, Design Zentrum North Rhine-Westphalia/D (for ›Context-Cut‹)
1974	Staatspreis für das Kunsthandwerk Rhineland-Palatinate/D	1999	Contemporary Design Group Award, Hall of Fame, Las Vegas/USA
1980	Distinction, Staatspreis für das Kunsthandwerk Rhineland-Palatinate/D	2001	Anerkennung für Produktdesign, Designpreis Rhineland-Palatinate/D
1981	1st prize, artists' competition ›Architektur-Kleinplastik‹, Mainz/D		
1981	Gold and bronze medals, Zlatarska Razstava Celjy/YUG		
1983	Honorary Membership, Worshipful Company of Goldsmiths, London/GB		
1984	1st and 2nd prizes, Deutscher Schmuck- und Edelsteinpreis, Idar-Oberstein/D		
1987	1st prize, Deutscher Schmuck- und Edelsteinpreis, Idar-Oberstein/D		
1992	1st prize, Prix Arctica, Kemi Art Museum, Kemi/FIN		

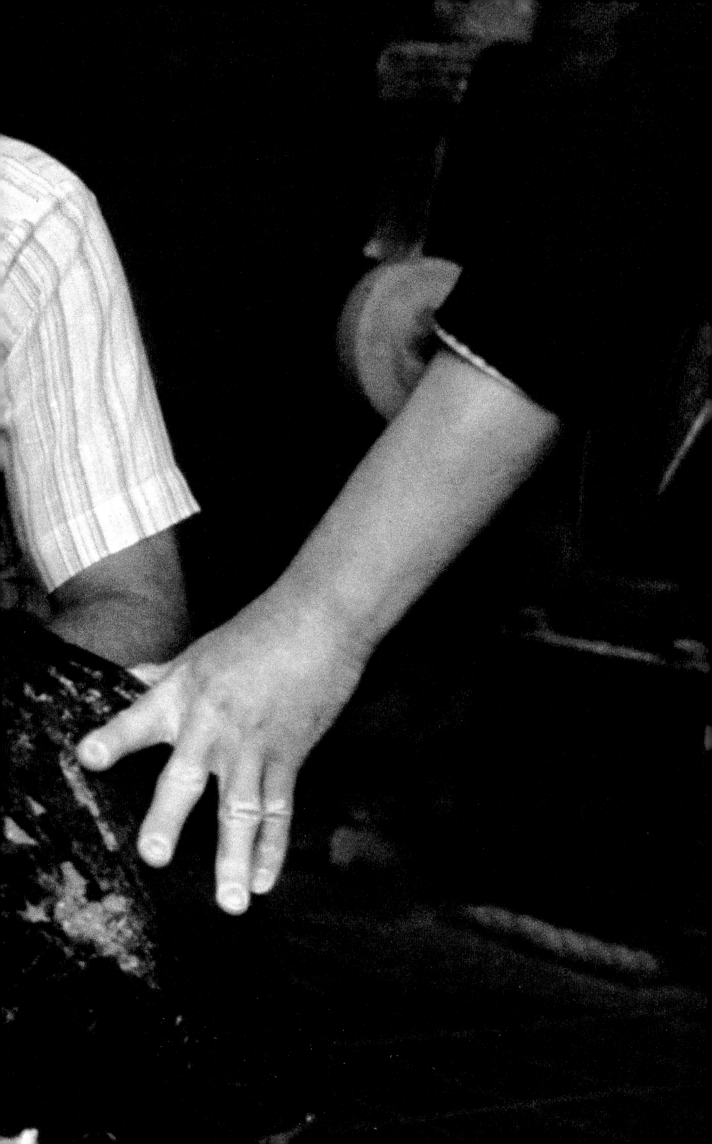

AUSSTELLUNGEN (AUSWAHL)
EXHIBITIONS (A SELECTION)

1968 Dortmund/D, Haus der Signal-Versicherungen

1969 Koblenz/D, Mittelrhein-Museum
Hameln/D, Kunstkreis »Neuer Schmuck«
København/DK, Galerie Hans Hansen
München/D, Galerie Handwerk

1970 Kaufbeuren-Neugablonz/D, Arbeitskreis Form
und Farbe
Düsseldorf/D, Galerie Orfèvre
Hameln/D, Kunstkreis »Neuer Schmuck 70«
Bremen/D, Focke-Museum, »Werkstoff und
Farbe«
Pforzheim/D, Schmuckmuseum, »Schmuck 70 –
Tendenzen«

1971 Mainz/D, Mittelrheinisches Landesmuseum
Höhr-Grenzhausen/D, »Objekte 71«
Ottawa/CDN, Robertson Galleries

1972 Hamburg, »Experimente«
Höhr-Grenzhausen/D, »Objekte 72«

1973 Höhr-Grenzhausen/D, »Objekte 73«

1974 Stuttgart/D, Jacobi, »Avantgarde 74«
Mainz/D, Römisch-Germanisches Zentralmu-
seum

1975 Hanau/D, Deutsches Goldschmiedehaus
Celjy/YUG, »Deutsche Schmuckausstellung«

1976 Höhr-Grenzhausen/D, »Objekte 76«
Bruxelles/B, Galerie Tabbah

1977 Koblenz/D, Mittelrhein-Museum
Bruxelles/B, Galerie L'Écuyer

1978 Höhr-Grenzhausen/D, »Objekte 78«

1979 Burgdorf/CH, Internationale Kunsthandwerk-
Ausstellung,
København/DK, Galerie for Nutidig Solv- og
Guldsmedekunst

1980 Höhr-Grenzhausen/D, »Objekte 80«
Mainz/D, Mittelrheinisches Landesmuseum
Höhr-Grenzhausen/D, Werkstattausstellung
Heiner Balzar

1981 Barcelona/E, Rosa Bisbe
Hong Kong, Hotel Peninsula, Golay-Buchel
San Francisco/USA, Contemporary Artisans
Gallery
Klagenfurt/A, Schmuckgalerie IBO

1982 Burgdorf/CH, Galerie Weber
Saarbrücken/D, Moderne Galerie

1983 Klagenfurt/A, Galerie IBO
San Francisco/USA, Contemporary Artisans
Gallery
Koblenz/D, Künstlerhaus Metternich
Höhr-Grenzhausen/D, »Objekte 83«

1985 New York/USA, Aaron Faber Gallery
San Francisco/USA, Elaine Potter Gallery
Paris/F, Musée du Luxembourg, »Material +
Form«
Mainz/D, Mittelrheinisches Landesmuseum,
»Material + Form«
Milano/I, Galleria Misami

1986 Strasbourg/F, »Exposition Cristaux 86«
Helsinki/FIN, Björn Weckström Gallery
Höhr-Grenzhausen/D, Keramikmuseum Wester-
wald, »Objekte 86«

1987 Dortmund/D, Museum für Naturkunde
Carmel/USA, Concepts Gallery
Palo Alto/USA, Concepts Gallery

1988 København/DK, Georg Jensen
Paris/F, Cité des Sciences et de l'Industrie,
»Bijoux«
New York/USA, H. Stern

1989 Bonn/D, Bundeskanzleramt, »Material + Form«
Lincoln/GB, Usher Gallery
London/GB, Barican Center
Trier/D, Landesmuseum
New York/USA Aaron Gaber Gallery

1990 Mannheim/D, Reiß-Museum, »Schmuck
Europa 90«
Höhr-Grenzhausen/D, Keramikmuseum Wester-
wald, »Objekte 90«
Paris/F, Université Pierre et Marie Curie, Collection
de Minéral
Helsinki/FIN, Konstindustrimuseet

1991 Dresden/D, Schloss Pillnitz, »Material + Form«
Andorra, Galeria del Mercat del Diamant
London/GB, Electrum Gallery

1992 Villach/A, Widmanneum
New York/USA, H. Stern, »The Cutting Edge«
Kaiserslautern, Pfalzgalerie, »Material + Form«

1993 Hanau/D, Deutsches Goldschmiedhaus, »Gruppe
Aspect's«
Beverly Hills, L.A./USA, Gallery Sculpture to
Wear

1994 Baden-Baden/D, Fritz-Walter-DFB-Pokal
Tokyo/J, Seibu Art Forum

1995 Zermatt/CH, Galerie Schindler
Palo Alto, C./USA, The Art of Goldsmithing, »DE
NOVO«
Firenze/I, Fallani Best
Hamburg/D, »Erotischer Schmuck im TRAXX«
Tokyo/J, Deutsche Botschaft, »Wein und Kunst
Rheinland-Pfalz«

BIBLIOGRAFIE (AUSWAHL)
BIBLIOGRAPHY (A SELECTION)

1996   Haigerloch/D, Schloss, »Erotischer Schmuck«
Idar-Oberstein/D, Museum Idar-Oberstein,
»500 Jahre Edelsteinbearbeitung«
Mainz/D, Landeszentralbank, »Edle Steine –
Kühne Gestalter«
Höhr-Grenzhausen/D, Keramikmuseum
Westerwald, »Objekte 71«
Roma/I, Bijoux et Pierres, »Oro ed Eros«
Seoul/South Corea, Tokyo/J, »Wein und Kunst
Rheinland-Pfalz«
Dubai/Emirate Dubai, »The Big 5 Show –
Land Rheinland-Pfalz«

1997   Essen/D, Design Zentrum Nordrhein-Westfalen,
»Selection«
Vail/USA, J. Cotter Gallery
New York/USA, Aaron Faber Gallery
Berlin/D, Galerie Dargo – New Jewellery + Art
Galerie im Hotel Adlon

1998   New York/USA, Aaron Faber Gallery
Santa Barbara/USA, Oliver & Espig Gallery
Berlin/D, Galerie Dargo – New Jewellery + Art
Galerie im Hotel Adlon

1999   Carlsbad, California/USA, Gemological Institute
of America, setting up the sculpture »Blue
Quartz Millenium«

2000   London/GB, Christie's, »Jewelry as Art«
San Francisco/USA, Revere Academy of Jewelry
Arts, Master Symposium
New York/USA, Aaron Faber Gallery
Sedona/USA, Exposures Gallery of Fine Art

2001   Bad Kreuznach/D, Schlossparkmuseum,
»Schmuckdesign und Objekte«
Barcelona/E, Galeria Nuria Ruiz, »Munsteiner's
Zeit«
Scottsdale/USA, Designer Jeweler French
Sedona/USA, Exposures Gallery of Fine Art

2002   Santa Ana, California/USA, Bowers Museum,
»Light and Stone, Michael Scott Collection«
Sedona/USA, Exposures Gallery of Fine Art

2003   Guebwiller/F, Musée du Florival
Höhr-Grenzhausen/D, Keramikmuseum Westerwald, Objekte 71

1974   Karl Schollmayer, Neuer Schmuck, Tübingen,
201–204

1982   Oppi Unbetracht, Jewelry Concepts and
Technology, New York, 592, 610

1983   Fachkunde Edelmetallgewerbe, 417

1984   Bijoux, Lausanne, 9–24

1985   Gottfried Borrmann, Kunsthandwerk
Rheinland-Pfalz, Mainz, 108, 178–180, 184

1992   Claude Mazloum (ed.), Designer Jewellery,
Roma, 26–37

1993   Claude Mazloum (ed.), L'Art de la Joaillerie
Contemporaine, Roma, 116–125
Claude Mazloum (ed.), Gioielli D'Arte, Roma,
116–125

1994   Bernd Munsteiner, Lausanne

1995   Mazloum, Claude (ed.): Schmuckverführungen,
Roma, 88–97

1999   Claude Mazloum (ed.), Edelsteine im 21. Jahr-
hundert/Jewelry Design in the 21st Century,
Roma, 26–37

2000   Munsteiner's Zeit, Barcelona

2001   Carlos Codina, Orfebreria, Barcelona, 88–93

2002   Michael M. Scott (ed.): Light & Stone.
Highlights from The Scott Gem Collection,
Santa Ana, 71–78

ABKÜRZUNGEN
ABBREVIATIONS

ct   Karat (1 ct = 0,2 g) || carat (1 ct = 0,2 g)
H   Höhe || height

© 2004 ARNOLDSCHE Art Publishers, Stuttgart, und die Autoren || and the authors

HERAUSGEBER || EDITOR
Wilhelm Lindemann

AUTOREN || AUTHORS
Deborah Aquado, Si + Ann Frazier, Wilhelm Lindemann, Michael M. Scott,
Dr. Christianne Weber-Stöber

KURZTEXTE || SHORT TEXTS
Wilhelm Lindemann (Seiten || pages 42–47, 49, 52, 101, 104, 129, 132, 165, 168)

REDAKTION || EDITORIAL WORK
Wilhelm Lindemann, Bernd Munsteiner, Winfried Stürzl (ARNOLDSCHE)

ÜBERSETZUNG INS ENGLISCHE || TRANSLATION FROM
GERMAN INTO ENGLISH
Joan Clough, München

ÜBERSETZUNG AUS DEM ENGLISCHEN || TRANSLATION FROM
ENGLISH INTO GERMAN
Saskia Breitling, Leipzig/Stuttgart (Texte || texts: Aquado, Frazier, Scott)

GRAFISCHE GESTALTUNG || LAYOUT
Silke Nalbach, Volker Kühn, nalbach typografik, Stuttgart

OFFSET-REPRODUKTIONEN || OFFSET-REPRODUCTIONS
Repromayer, Reutlingen

DRUCK || PRINTING
Leibfarth & Schwarz, Dettingen/Erms

Dieses Buch wurde gedruckt auf 100% chlorfrei gebleichtem Papier und
entspricht damit dem TCF-Standard.
This book has been printed on paper that is 100% free of chlorine bleach in
conformity with TCF standards.

Bibliografische Information Der Deutschen Bibliothek
Die Deutsche Bibliothek verzeichnet diese Publikation in der Deutschen
Nationalbibliografie; detaillierte bibliografische Daten sind im Internet über
http://dnb.ddb.de abrufbar.
Bibliographic information published by Die Deutsche Bibliothek
Die Deutsche Bibliothek lists this publication in the Deutsche Nationalbibli-
ografie; detailed bibliographic data is available in the Internet at
http://dnb.ddb.de.

ISBN 3-89790-203-6

Made in Germany, 2004

UMSCHLAG || COVER
Bernd Munsteiner, »Reflektierende Perspektiven«, 1992, Turmalin 113,89 ct,
Michael M. Scott Collection (siehe auch S. 115)
Bernd Munsteiner, »Reflecting Perspectives«, 1992, tourmaline 113.89 ct,
Michael M. Scott Collection (see also p. 115)

BILDNACHWEIS || PHOTO CREDITS
Archiv Munsteiner: 220/221
Bibliothèque Nationale, Paris (fol. 137): 23
Werner Baumann, Höhr-Grenzhausen: 9, 44, 54–58, 60, 77, 79, 80, 82, 200,
201, 204
Jürgen Cullmann (Lichtblick), Schwollen: 28, 29, 34, 36, 37, 42–47, 50/51, 53,
59, 61–71, 77, 78, 81, 82, 84–91, 93, 94, 107, 110–113, 115, 118–123,
125, 126, 128, 130/131, 133, 135, 138–142, 144, 145, 147, 149, 152, 153,
156, 157, 159–164, 169, 171–176, 181, 184–189, 196, 203, 205, 207,
209–211, 214, 215, Cover
© Domkapitel Aachen (Foto: Ann Münchow): 15
Rudolf Dröschel, Idar-Oberstein: 25
Gemmological Institute of America, Carlsbad, California/USA: 183, 212
Ludger Grunwald, Berlin: 1, 2–9, 202, 213
Herzog-August-Bibliothek, Wolfenbüttel (Cod. Guelf. 1.9 Aug. 2°, 68 recto): 17
Hessische Landes- und Hochschulbibliothek Darmstadt (Sign. Rf.16): 21
H.P. Hoffmann, Düsseldorf: 127
Lorne Liesenfeld, Warschau: 139, 141, 156–158, 169, 175, 186, 206, 214
Rheinisches Bildarchiv Köln (Schnütgenmuseum Köln, Inv.-Nr. G 17): 17
Schmuckmuseum Pforzheim (Foto: Rüdiger Flöter, Pforzheim): 199
Städtische Galerie im Lenbachhaus, München (Inv.-Nr. G 13320): 194
Ständebuch Jost Ammans, Frankfurt am Main, 1568: 21
Erica Van Pelt, Los Angeles: 32, 33, 39, 40, 44, 46, 83, 95–98, 100, 102/103,
105, 109, 116, 117, 124, 139, 143, 148, 150, 151, 154, 155, 166/167, 187,
206, 208
© Wenzel-Hablik-Stiftung, Itzehoe: 192, 193
Michael Zobel, Konstanz: 197

© VG Bild-Kunst, Bonn 2004: 195 (Mitte), 197 (rechts)

REPRODUKTIONEN AUS || REPRODUCTIONS FROM
195: Bruno Taut, Frühlicht, 1920
24: Jean-Baptiste Tavernier 1984, S. 190 (vgl. Anm. 18, S. 41)
26: Herbert Tillander 1995, S. 175–177 (vgl. Anm. 19, S. 41)

DANK || ACKNOWLEDGEMENTS
Stadt Idar-Oberstein
Landkreis Birkenfeld
Ministerium für Wissenschaft, Weiterbildung, Forschung und Kultur Rheinland-Pfalz
Museumsverband Rheinland-Pfalz
Scott Gem Collection
Kreissparkasse Birkenfeld

BESONDERER DANK AN || SPECIAL THANKS TO
Hannelore Munsteiner
Jutta Munsteiner
Tom Munsteiner